# CREATING AND PRESENTING
# An Early Childhood Education
# PORTFOLIO

A Reflective Approach

# CREATING AND PRESENTING
# An Early Childhood Education
# PORTFOLIO

A Reflective Approach

First Edition

by

## DELORES LOWE FRIEDMAN, ED. D.

Professor of Early Childhood Education

Kingsborough Community College of the City University of New York

**WADSWORTH**
CENGAGE Learning™

Australia • Brazil • Japan • Korea • Mexico • Singapore • Spain • United Kingdom • United States

**Creating and Presenting An Early Childhood Education Portfolio: A Reflective Approach, First Edition**
Delores Lowe Friedman, Ed. D.

Publisher: Linda Schreiber-Ganster

Executive Editor: Mark Kerr

Assistant Editor: Caitlin Cox

Editorial Assistant/Associate: Genevieve Allen

Marketing Manager: Kara Kindstrom

Marketing Assistant/Associate: Dimitri Hagnere

Marketing Communications Manager: Tami Strang

Content Project Management: PreMediaGlobal

Art Director: Jennifer Wahi

Manufacturing Buyer: Becky Cross

Manufacturing Manager: Marcia Locke

Rights Acquisitions Specialist: Roberta Broyer

Rights Acquisitions Director: Bob Kauser

Cover Designer: Marsha Cohen

Cover Image: Getty images/Blend Images/ Ariel Skelley

Compositor: PreMediaGlobal

For product information and technology assistance, contact us at **Cengage Learning Customer & Sales Support, 1-800-354-9706**

For permission to use material from this text or product, submit all requests online at **cengage.com/permissions** Further permissions questions can be emailed to **permissionrequest@cengage.com**

Library of Congress Control Number: 2010941138

ISBN-13: 978-1-111-34433-7

ISBN-10: 1-111-34433-7

**Wadsworth**
20 Davis Drive
Belmont, CA 94002-3098
USA

Cengage Learning is a leading provider of customized learning solutions with office locations around the globe, including Singapore, the United Kingdom, Australia, Mexico, Brazil, and Japan. Locate your local office at: **international.cengage.com/region**

Cengage Learning products are represented in Canada by Nelson Education, Ltd.

For your course and learning solutions, visit **www.cengage.com**

Purchase any of our products at your local college store or at our preferred online store **www.cengagebrain.com**

Printed in the United States of America
1 2 3 4 5 6 7 15 14 13 12 11 10

# About the Author

Delores Lowe Friedman, Ed. D., is professor of early childhood education at Kingsborough Community College of the City University of New York, where she teaches courses in early childhood education, curriculum, and supervises student field experience. She has served as a consultant on early childhood philosophy and methods and parent involvement to the New York City Department of Education's Early Childhood and Elementary Education Office, many school districts in the greater New York area, regional training offices for Head Start, and for Bank Street College of Education.

Dr. Friedman was honored at Kingsborough Community College with a president's Innovation Award for her program, Power Up: From Binder to e-Portfolio, and is heading an initiative that engages early childhood education students in reflection on their binder portfolios and developing e-portfolios. Dr. Friedman was honored by the Chancellor of the City University of New York as the recipient of three major institutional grants: one from the National Science Foundation for the preparation of pre-service teachers in science, math and technology education; a Goals 2000 grant for the professional development of teachers in New York City public schools; and a Workforce Development grant for the career development of teachers in early care and education.

Dr. Friedman is the author of scholarly articles in journals such as the *Journal of College Science Teaching,* and *Young Children,* the journal of the National Association for the Education of Young Children and *The Clearing House*. She holds a doctorate from Teachers College, Columbia University where she has had the honor of serving as the President of the Teachers College Alumni Council. Her dissertation, New York State's Policy on Parent Involvement: From Concept to Implementation was on the New York State Board of Regents parent involvement policy entitled "Parent Partnerships: Linking Families, Communities and Schools." She served as the primary author of this document and project manager of the policy making process when she was an Associate in the Office of Parent Education, Child and Student Development Services, of the New York State Education Department. She holds New York State Certification as a School District Administrator.

Dr. Friedman has authored numerous children's books, which promote early literacy, multicultural education, and a love of science and math.

Her professional affiliations include the National Association for the Education of Young Children, The Association for Authentic, Experiential and Evidence-Based Learning (AAEEBL), The National Science Teachers Association, and ASCD (formerly the Association for Supervision and Curriculum Development).

# Dedication

I dedicate this book to my family with my love:

My husband, Karl, for his love and support for this work
and all of my projects; and

My mother, Louise, and my sister, Barbara, for their constancy
and encouragement; and

My son, Ian, for his technological expertise, his thoughtfulness
and generosity of spirit.

# Table of Contents

## SECTION II   Reflection and Your Portfolio    27

### CHAPTER 3   First Reflections and Your Portfolio    29

## CHAPTER 7    The e-Portfolio    112

# Preface

The intent of this book is to provide practical guidance to early childhood education students as they prepare portfolios of their work. It is the intent of the book to help students understand what a portfolio is and what it can do for them. It also shows students how to shape and develop the portfolio in a way that serves their professional and educational goals.

Conversations with two students and my observations of the portfolio process prompted me to write this book. The first student told me about a job interview she had for a position as a Head Start teacher. I was surprised to learn that eight to ten people interviewed her, and I began asking her questions about her experience. She told me that that upon her arrival at the interview, she was escorted into a conference room where she was seated at a table with several other people. There were two directors (regional and center), two teachers, parents, and the social worker. Seeing that many people made my student nervous and, to stay composed, she busied herself with taking out her portfolio and placing it in front of her. She said it was the smartest thing she could have done, because at the outset one interviewer asked her what it was. She told them it was a portfolio of her work, and they asked to see it. Then they passed it around and, as they flipped through the pages, they asked her about various pieces of work in it. She felt instantly at ease, because she was intimately aware of all of her work, and she could talk extemporaneously about each piece. She told about her lessons—their strengths and things she would improve. She told about observations of children she had done, and what she had learned about child development and teaching from them. The interview was a success.

The second student was one who had long graduated and gotten both her bachelor's and master's degrees. She had been teaching for about ten years. I asked if she remembered her portfolio, because I thought that I might write about portfolios. She said, "I not only remember it, I took it to my first job interview with a principal. He later told me that it was the reason he hired me. I still have it and I still use it." It now held work that she used in her fourth-grade teaching, but early on it held material from her years as a kindergarten teacher. She explained that each year she revised it, taking out materials, storing some in a file cabinet, and putting in materials that she might use in her current teaching assignment.

What these students learned was the power of the portfolio as a tool in demonstrating their growth, archiving and organizing their work, showcasing their successes, informing their practice, and improving themselves as early childhood professionals. However, each semester, as the end of the term nears, when instructors ask to see students' portfolios, the students engage in a panicked rush to look at others' portfolios, and put work into their portfolios sometimes without the care and thought that the process deserves. Our program and its portfolio process has evolved over time. Twenty years ago, it was more of a scrapbook containing student work, articles, and resources. It has grown into a more supervised, compendium of student work drawn from each of their courses. Missing was a cohesive process where the students could take control of building the portfolio from beginning to end, with an understanding of why certain artifacts or sections, and pieces should be brought together, based on the students' own ideas and reflections on teaching and learning.

As I researched the portfolio-building process, there were certain steps that were spoken of in the literature and some elements that I wanted to include as a constructivist educator. I wanted to help students to become active participants in the process of creating a portfolio. I wanted to actively engage students in collecting their work, purposefully selecting the pieces, reflecting upon them, and presenting the work that they would produce. In addition, however, I wanted to give students a reflective process for selecting their work that they could use throughout their careers.

As I prepared this manuscript, I was mindful of the theoretical underpinnings I wanted the book to convey. I wanted it to be constructivist in nature, in that I wanted students to be engaged in the "doing" or constructing of the portfolio from an experiential perspective. I wanted the approach, throughout the book, to be on the reflections of the students on their experiences that give their work meaning. So throughout the book there are reflective tasks that help students to present their thinking about teaching and learning. Their understandings about our profession are what will make their portfolios meaningful to their own self-evaluation and growth as teachers. Their reflections will also be what will make their portfolios unique and memorable to a reader. I also wanted the book to help students to use the standards developed by the National Association for the Education of Young Children to assess their work, and guide their rationales for selecting work for inclusion.

This book was designed to give students the skills that will enable them to:

- develop a portfolio for self-assessment using the latest NAEYC standards;
- create a portfolio to showcase their best work and their reflective analysis;
- present their work in an e-portfolio making it accessible on the Internet;
- become engaged in a reflective process for developing dynamic portfolios—binders or e-portfolios—that will grow with them and serve them throughout their years as early childhood professionals.

## ORGANIZATION

The book is organized to assist students in the development of their portfolio from a developmental point of view. It is intended to guide an early childhood student, step by step, through the process of building their portfolios.

In designing the portfolio guide, I was mindful of the fact that so often students are working on their portfolios alone. They bring in their binders or share their e-portfolios and then get feedback from their instructors. We tell them to "Take this out" or "Put that in." I wanted the student to be more aware of what should go in and why, and so this book is intended to provide a structure for students to follow as they develop their portfolios. Although many guides give information about what a portfolio is, and what it contains, few guides walk students through the reflective process of actually building the portfolio step by step. The advantage of this guide is that it is designed to help students develop their portfolios in an orderly way. This is a reflective process, once learned, that students can use to analyze their work for the rest of their professional careers.

This book is organized into four sections.

1. In Section One students get a foundation of information about portfolios.

2. In Section Two, students are engaged in learning about reflection and beginning a process of reflective thinking they will use as they build their portfolios.

3. In Section Three, the students will construct their portfolios testing each artifact using the "Three-Question Rationale Test," and then select their work and present it in the portfolio.

4. Section Four provides information on finishing up the portfolio-making process, giving tips on flagging items and creating summary documents.

## FEATURES

As you thumb through this book you will notice some key features designed to assist students in the portfolio-making process.

**Checklists** You will find checklists at the beginning and/or end of each chapter. Those at the beginning are there to signal needed materials for the work in the chapter. Checklists at the end are there to help students review what they have accomplished in that chapter.

**Tasks Icon** The Task Icon signals a portfolio-building task in the text. These tasks include basic steps such as selecting the portfolio type and organizing artifacts, as well as reflective tasks that will help students gain an understanding of themselves, the portfolio-making process, or an artifact, as well as teaching and learning.

**Rationale Tests** The Three-Question Rationale Test guides students in assessing their artifacts (observations, lesson plans, curriculum projects, research papers) by describing the work, holding it up to the NAEYC

Standards, and noting what it is that they have learned by doing the work. By answering the three-question test, students will also be drafting their rationale statements.

**Example and Samples** Throughout the book we provide examples of the documents we expect the students to develop, including sample Autobiographies, Teaching Philosophy Statements, and Professional Goal Statements, Rationale Statements, Cover Pages, and E-portfolio screenshots to give students an example to guide them in executing these documents for their portfolios.

**Artifact Lists** An extensive list of potential artifacts students might include in their portfolios.

**Artifact Index Sheets** are provided to be used to keep track of the portfolio-building process as artifacts are selected and included.

## INTERNET RESOURCES

The Book Companion website at www.cengage.com/education/Friedman provides online templates of Reflective Task questions to a support student's creation of Autobiographies, Teaching Philosophy, Portfolio Purpose Statement, Professional Goals Statement, and Rationale Statements.

**Website templates** are provided of the various reflective tasks in the book, so that students can simply respond to the questions on the online template, easily composing their Portfolio Purpose Statement, Autobiographies, Teaching Philosophy, Professional Goals Statement, and Rationale Statements. Additional curriculum-related Autobiographies are also provided so that students might develop their own Science Autobiography, Social Studies Autobiography, Music Autobiography, Art Autobiography, etc. We provided these because we know that student's early experiences with curriculum areas usually help to form their foundational views of curricula. These artifacts very often inform their views about teaching and learning in a curricular area, and are significant to the developing body of work collected as a teacher.

## A SPECIAL NOTE TO THE STUDENT

This book is intended as a guide through the portfolio-building process. You will be asked to reflect on issues, which will move you, step by step, through the process of preparing the portfolio. The reflective tasks may contain questions, which are intended to help you to understand either yourself or the portfolio-making process, or to develop an element of the portfolio. The questions should never be limiting, but rather opportunities for you to think about the topic at hand. You should pursue any additional ideas, thoughts, and reflections you may have, which were stimulated by a particular question(s). Write everything down. Your thoughts and ideas about yourself, about teaching and learning, and about children and their development are important to this process and should be respected.

## A NOTE TO THE INSTRUCTOR/FACILITATOR

This book is a guide to assist you in your work with students as they produce a portfolio. It is not intended as a lock-step script. It is an open process that will lead students in the construction of their portfolios. Just as I have asked your students not to limit their thinking to only the specific questions in this guide, I invite you to add questions that you would like students to consider as they reflect on artifacts that they are analyzing or producing for their portfolios.

The reflection tasks, with questions in this book, are intended to scaffold the writing process for students. You can also use these questions for a group to consider together after an individual engages in reflective writing. Small group discussions, about some of these questions, can help students to share ideas, gain different perspectives, and develop collegial relationships around portfolio building. The give and take in these discussions can strengthen the sense of community students feel as they grow together as professionals.

# Acknowledgments

I thank the following people and groups for their support in the development of this book. First, I would like to acknowledge Kingsborough Community College, of the City University of New York, President Regina Peruggi, Provost Stuart Suss, and, Dr. William Burger, Chair of the Department of Behavioral Sciences for supporting the sabbatical during which I did the preliminary work on this book. I would like to thank the City University of New York and the Professional Staff Congress for making this sabbatical support available to me and other faculty who pursue research. I would also like to thank them and Associate Provost Reza Fakhari, and the President's Faculty Innovation Award Committee for that award, which supported experimental work on e-portfolio development at Kingsborough Community College.

I would like to give a special thank you to my colleagues at Kingsborough Community College for their support of my e-portfolio project; Vice President David Gomez for his continued support of my project and other technology in education projects; and Dr. Michael Rosson, Director of the Kingsborough Center for Advanced Technology Training (KCATT), Professor Christoph Winkler of the Faculty Interest Group in Technology and Education, and my colleagues in the e-Portfolio Faculty Interest Group, for the give and take. I also want to thank those colleagues in the Early Childhood Education Program, who supported my e-portfolio project.

I would like to thank the National Association for the Education of Young Children for their permission to quote from the policy document: NAEYC Standards for Early Childhood Professional Preparation Programs (2009). I invite the readers of the book to seek the full text of the NAEYC documents referenced here at www.NAEYC.org.

I want to thank Jeffrey Yan of Digication, for permitting me to use screen shots of students' e-portfolios, and my students, Joy Martin, Veronica Mc Tigue, Dominic Jenkins, and Marilyn Ricco, for allowing me to publish screenshots of parts of their e-portfolios.

I would like to thank my son, Ian L. Friedman, a software engineer, for his technological expertise and support throughout this project at any time of the night or day. His ideas about software, hardware, and use of the Internet have helped me to do this work better and with greater efficiency.

I want to thank Christine Rose Pollice for her contributions to my e-portfolio project.

I want to thank my very good friends, Myrna Rivera, Nancy Mintz, Dean Fern Khan of Bank Street College, Professor Suzanne Carothers of New York University, and Rose Ranieri Crosby, who were there to listen and support me throughout.

I want to acknowledge my husband Karl M. Friedman, who was always there to discuss ideas, read and reread chapters, and encourage and support me in every project I pursue.

I want to thank my editor, Caitlin Cox and her team for shepherding this project through to completion.

I want to thank the trailblazers in the field of e-portfolios, especially Dr. Helen Barrett, whose generosity in making her work available and providing forums for sharing experiences, and despite her busy schedule making time to answer a question about the practical application of e-portfolios.

Finally, I want to thank those who participated in the reviews that helped shape this book.

Cheryl Cranston, Association of Christian Schools International
Amber Tankersley, University of Arkansas Child Development Center
Alice D. Beyrent, Hesser College
Priscilla Smith, Gwinnett Technical College
Gail Hartin, Southern Methodist University
Brenda McFarland, Isothermal Community College
Teresa Thompson, Butler Community College
Sabine Gerhardt, University of Akron
Nancy Spurgeon, Wenatchee Valley College
Tina Suarez, Kaskaskia College
Jill Harrison, Delta College
Joan Parris, Norwalk Community College
Sharon R. Calhoun, Cuyahoga Community College
Mary Svoboda-Chollet, Metropolitan Community College—Penn Valley

Mary Jane Eisenhauer, Purdue University North Central
Rusty Barrier, New Brighton Institute
Sheila Rowland, Oklahoma State University
Gayle Dilling, Olympic College
Marilyn Cavazos, Laredo Community College
Tiffany Wright, Monroe County Community College
Christine Lux, Montana State University
Elizabeth P. Quintero, California State University Channel Islands
Lee Alvoid, Southern Methodist University
Heidi Frankard, Metropolitan State University
Joyce Hargrove, Phillips Community College of the University of Arkansas
Caroline Clark-Murphy, Northwest Missouri State University
Marilyn Chu, Ed. D., Western Washington University
Mary Ursits, Kennesaw State University
Sharon Little, South Piedmont Community College
Mary Lou Calvert Forman, Ashland Community and Technical College
Susan Baxter, Sampson Community College
Stanley R. Stephens, West Georgia Technical College
Ron Mihalko, East Stroudsburg University
Diane Ward, Roane State Community College
Trude Puckett, Pulaski Technical College
Sherry Fairfield-Tagle, Muskegon Community College
Elizabeth Persons, Pensacola State College

# Your Teaching Portfolio: What? Why? How?

In this section you will find out about the "nuts and bolts" of developing a portfolio. You will learn:

- what teaching portfolios are;

- why, and how, you can use them;

- the different types of portfolios you can create;

- how to organize a portfolio, and what to put into it.

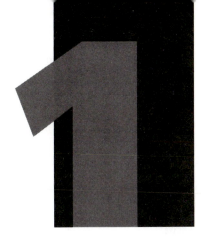

# What Is a Portfolio and Why Do I Need One?

"Portfolios are students' own stories of what they know, why they believe they know it, and why others should be of the same opinion."

From **"Portfolios: Stories of Knowing"** Paulson & Paulson (1991)

We have all seen a model, carrying a large black leather portfolio in tow as she goes to class, to auditions, or to work. The materials in the portfolio may be such things as her photographs that demonstrate the various kinds of modeling work of which she is capable—catalog, high fashion, etc. She has her resume, which tells us what work she has done. There is usually some kind of goal or job objective statement telling us the work for which she is currently looking. Just as the model's portfolio demonstrates her capability and past work, a teaching portfolio represents you as a teacher, your goals, your skills, your philosophy of teaching, and evidence of your past work.

Many educators in this field define a portfolio this way, "A portfolio is a purposeful collection of student work that exhibits the student's efforts, progress and achievements in one or more areas. . . ." (Paulson, Paulson and Mayer, 1991). Your teaching portfolio, then, is a collection of your work and your reflections or thoughts about your work.

Your portfolio is a dynamic, evolving record of who you are as a teacher. Because your portfolio documents your work and your reflection or thinking about your work, your portfolio can showcase your work for employers and for further education. It will contain **artifacts** or pieces of work that demonstrate your planning such as lesson and unit plans. It will include evidence of your abilities with observing and recording children's behavior, such as a child study. It will include various certificates, which substantiate your knowledge and skills, such as a certificate, which prepares you for recognizing and reporting child abuse and neglect. Your portfolio is where you will collect the work that represents you as a professional. It will say what you have learned, and what you can do as an early childhood professional.

Your reflections or thoughts about your work are important because they tell what you have learned from your perspective. Your understanding about what you have learned will help you and anyone who looks at your portfolio know what you take away from the work experience, and its meaning to you. It also helps you to think about the future challenges and opportunities for which this piece of learning has prepared you. In other words, now that you have learned what you have in this context, what new learning experiences are you seeking in the future.

Because your portfolio represents you and your capabilities, it can help you accomplish major objectives such as:

- constructing knowledge about yourself as a teacher;
- monitoring your growth and development;
- dialoguing with your professors about your development;
- showcasing your best work.

## Constructing Knowledge About Yourself as a Teacher

As an early childhood education student, you have learned about constructivism and student-centered learning. Constructivism is the philosophy of learning that suggests that children/learners construct their own knowledge. The child/learner gains experience and through talking, writing, drawing, or building, reconstructs that knowledge. With the student at the center of learning we encourage the learner to make choices, to explore materials, and to problem solve. As early childhood teachers, we want students to gain experience and construct their understandings about the world. Creating a portfolio is a constructivist activity in which you will be constructing knowledge about yourself as a teacher. You will make choices about what work of yours is representative of your thinking and your skills and abilities. You will, as you look at each piece of work, engage with what was learned in the work, and how it has changed you. You will necessarily think about what you have learned that has remained a part of who you now are as a teacher. You will also begin to think about what more you want to know as a teacher, and how you still need to grow.

As you analyze your work to decide whether it should be included in your portfolio, you will be thinking about how this work relates to you and your understandings about teaching and learning. You will be testing the work against your growing beliefs and values. Ask yourself, does it meet the standards I am trying to attain? As you go through this process of reflecting about what you have learned and putting it into words, you will be constructing knowledge about yourself as a teacher. As you write your reasons or rationales for including pieces of work, you will be saying this is important because it is part of what I have learned, and part of what I believe as a professional. You will be constructing the story of your knowledge and belief systems as a teacher.

## Self-assessment: Monitoring Your Growth

A portfolio helps you to assess your own growth as a professional. Self-assessment is an important skill, because, if you can monitor your own growth, you can take a proactive role in preparing yourself for the future challenges and rewards of your career. You will not be waiting for a supervisor or college advisor to say you need to take a course, or develop a particular skill or ability. By monitoring your own progress, you will be planning the courses and preparation you need in an active way. Taking control of your career and planning the steps you take, will help you to move ahead in a deliberative way. It gives you power, because you are making the decisions about your own preparation.

The process of collecting materials, and selecting the work to use in your portfolio is also a way of documenting your reflections about your work. As you select pieces of work to include in your portfolio, you naturally engage in evaluating it. You reflect on what you did, and how you might improve upon it. You will also reflect on how the work meets the standards set by your college or the certifying authority in your state. (We will talk in greater depth about connecting to the standards later.) You will measure your growth against standards that are set for you by your college, your state, or a national professional certification organization. Depending on the standards by which your work will be judged, you may be asked to write a rationale, which tells why a particular piece of work helps you meet those standards. Your portfolio, and the work you do, as you develop it, will be a vital tool in helping you to be aware of the standards you are striving to reach as a teacher. It will help you to assess how the work you are doing helps you to meet the standards that are set for you. It helps you to be mindful of the areas in which you still need to work to develop the professional abilities required of you as a teacher.

At the beginning, this may seem like a daunting task, but you are not alone. If you think about it, you will have plenty of support. First, you will be able to track your own growth. You will learn to be your own best teacher, because you have your own best interest at heart. Your professors, and field supervisors, and cooperating teachers, and professional colleagues, such as your directors and staff developers all can be a great support. They want to see you grow because your development means their development as well. Your classmates and colleagues can also be a great support. As you talk about your portfolio with classmates, you may hear ideas about materials you should present that you had not thought of including. This book will also be a support, by helping you to build the portfolio piece by piece, and to engage in reflection in an organized way.

## Basis for Dialogue About Your Growth with Professors, Directors, and Staff Developers

As you work in your courses in early childhood education, you will be able to use your portfolio as the basis for conferences with your professors, field supervisors, directors, and staff developers. They will have ideas on the individual pieces of work you submit to them and the ways in which it might be improved. They will also have ideas on the pieces of work that might be done to move you to the next developmental level in your teaching. For example, let's say you did a small group science activity with children observing snow melting, your field supervisor might have you develop a web on the topic to develop follow-up activities for exploring liquids turning to solids. This might be the beginning stages of creating a unit. Developing a unit means thinking about how to build upon the understandings children gained from the individual lesson. By doing this next level of work, and documenting it, you will demonstrate your professional growth and development. The portfolio artifact is the focus of the discussion that moves you to that next level of development.

Your portfolio is a dynamic, growing, and changing representation of you as a teacher. At some point, your professors will want to consult with you about the entire body of work in your portfolio as it has been developed up to that point. They will be looking at the artifacts you have collected. They will be reading the rationales you have written to demonstrate why this piece of work helps to show your professional growth in meeting a standard. They may suggest that certain earlier work should now be removed. They may suggest that other lessons done more recently be included. They may feel that your self-evaluations of lessons should be rewritten to demonstrate the best thinking about the work you have done. They may say that the rationale needs tweaking, to better discuss the connection between the work and the standard. They may suggest including an additional standard that you may have met, but had not mentioned. Having the actual portfolio there as you have this dialogue, gives you concrete materials to discuss. It provides another perspective to help you to make the best decisions about the work that will help you to grow and develop, and demonstrate your growth to others.

## Teacher Preparation, Certification, and Licensure Requirement

The National Association for the Education of Young Children (NAEYC) and the National Council for the Accreditation of Teacher Education (NCATE) have set the standards for teacher preparation in early childhood education. Performance-based assessment or portfolio assessment is now an important part of how colleges and universities examine the skills and abilities novice teachers bring to teaching. Many states require teaching portfolios as part of their requirements for state certification. Your college should be aware of the particular standards and requirements you will have to fulfill, to become a certified teacher in your state. But you should become familiar with these requirements yourself. Most states have state education departments, which have such requirements on a website where you can read an online file on the standards that you must meet and the documentation that you must collect.

For licensing you will have to select the specific pieces that your college, or state licensing authority requires. Then you will prepare and submit it in the format that they require. Many institutions are now requiring the *e*-Portfolio, which we will describe in greater detail later in the chapter. Some require a CD of your work, and some may require a videotape of teaching and hard copy of lesson plans, evidence of student (children's) work, and your analyses of the work you have done. You will be required to provide documentation that is representative of your abilities at the end of the degree-granting process to receive licensure. What the university or the state is looking for are those capstone projects that best show your teaching abilities and your professionalism.

## To Showcase Your Work

The portfolio is the place where you demonstrate your skills as a teacher, and showcase your work. You may wish to showcase your work for future employers, graduate school admission, and certification with government or professional organizations. Teachers must know and understand child development, and how it relates to classroom practice. Your understandings about curriculum and its relationship to the ways in which you engage children are important indicators of how well you teach. So, your observations of children, your child studies, lesson plans, and unit plans, are all work that is demonstrative of your skills and abilities. Additionally, putting things in your portfolio requires you to do another level of thinking about how the artifacts relate to the standards in teaching that you must meet. You, therefore, get a chance to showcase your work, and to tell why you feel it is promoting the teaching standards to which you aspire.

## A Portfolio Is Not a Scrapbook

Because a portfolio is a compilation of artifacts, there is the tendency to view it as a scrapbook. Students, who see the portfolio this way, can seriously misjudge as it relates to the best choice of artifacts, their preparation, and presentation. The portfolio is not a random compendium of your work decorated with stickers, borders, and clever sayings. It is a serious place for presenting yourself as a professional to the world. It should show your depth as a thinking, skilled teacher, who is able to observe and assess a child's development, arrange a room, plan a lesson and a unit, and evaluate the success of your teaching. You need to be able to reflect on these practices, and think analytically about what you do as a teacher. You need to demonstrate the ways in which what you have learned about child development theory and practice has resulted in the practices that you have adopted. You must also demonstrate that when you needed to shift and change a practice that was not working, you had the capability to correct course, and adapt and change.

What you need to think about when preparing your portfolio is whether the work is professionally presented and organized in a way that makes sense to the reviewer. The work should be aesthetically pleasing, but focused upon the ideas. It should not be random, but have an organization that makes logical sense to the reader. They want to see a professionally prepared body of work, which represents you as a developing teacher.

There are three basic kinds of portfolios of which you as a pre-service teacher should be aware:

The Developmental Portfolio;

The Capstone or Showcase Portfolio;

The e-Portfolio.

## The Developmental Portfolio

The Developmental Portfolio is the portfolio you will be developing from the beginning of your work, which prepares you for teaching until licensure. This portfolio is called developmental, because it represents your development throughout the time you are learning your craft as a teacher. This developmental portfolio will document the entire process of your becoming a teacher. Because it will represent two to four years of work, it will be best kept in a large binder. (We will discuss the organization and preparation of the documents later in this section.)

This portfolio will contain the papers submitted to professors, tests, certificates earned (CDA, Child Abuse and Neglect), and any special training you have received which improves your abilities as a teacher. Your early work will be autobiographical reflections.

You may have early observational papers of children. Later work will include lesson plans and units. You will include your observations, lesson plans, unit plans, and any evaluations, analyses, and reflections on practice you have made in connection to this work. You can, and should, include evidence of children's work connected with these lessons, and any videos of the lessons, or digital photographs of the activities that you have taken.

You will also include a rationale or reason for the inclusion of each artifact. Your rationales will give the reader an idea of the purpose of the work, and how it addresses the goals and standards for teacher preparation set by your college or university. This rationale is also supposed to represent your thinking about how the work has helped you develop the skills and abilities you are striving for as a teacher.

## The Showcase or Capstone Portfolio

The Showcase or Capstone portfolio contains those few pieces of work that illustrate the best representation of you as a professional. In consultation with your professor, you will select the specific items. As you and your professor assess the work in your developmental portfolio you will be asking yourself two questions:

- What is the work that best represents my abilities as a teacher?
- What work most clearly represents my ability to meet the standards by which I am being evaluated?

Typically a capstone portfolio contains one of the very best lessons or units that you have done along with the analyses of your work, and reflections on how you might have improved it. A videotape or digitized record of the lesson may be required. It will also contain a child study, conducted over time, with reflections on what you have learned about the specific child, and child development. Major projects related to parent and/or community involvement or research papers on issues might also be included. The key is that the work selected should be the very best evidence of your abilities as a teacher.

### The e-Portfolio

The e-portfolio is an electronic representation of your portfolio or a digital record of your work. You can create an e-portfolio that is a developmental portfolio, or a showcase/capstone portfolio. In the e-portfolio, your artifacts are digitized and uploaded to a computer and a server. Advances in technology now allow for a state-of-the-art e-portfolio to be created for portfolio preparation. Many colleges and universities are moving toward helping their students demonstrate not only their best work as a teacher, but also their proficiency in the use of technology. An e-portfolio allows you to collect work for display, to reflect on that work, and store copies of documents such as certificates and licenses. You can use digital photos, digital video and sound to illustrate your artifacts.

The e-portfolio is dynamic because the user can create a variety of presentations for different audiences on the site. A portfolio that contains materials for an employer can be assembled to give only a resume, and a sample lesson with video and examples of children's work. Or, you can prepare a presentation that includes research papers, lessons, and unit plans, for a graduate school. Also, over time, you can add to the e-portfolio, updating it to grow with you.

An e-portfolio makes your portfolio more portable because it can be made available on the Internet or on CD or DVD. Unlike the binder portfolio, which is bulky and is usually carried to an employer or college or university, the e-portfolio can be accessed on the web, which makes it available to anyone worldwide.

## Finding Your Focus

Now that you have learned about portfolios, you need to find the focus of your work. Here are some questions to consider:

1. Why are you creating a portfolio?

2. What kind of portfolio will you create (developmental, showcase/capstone, e-portfolio)?

3. What is the benefit to you of creating that type of portfolio?

## Your Research for Chapter 2

Inquire of your professors whether they require a particular organizational method for portfolios. Look at binders of students who are further along in their education than you are. Make note of how they have organized their work. Find out what standards or competencies your college program, university, or state require for teacher preparation and obtain a copy.

## Concluding Remarks

The Chinese philosopher, Lao-Tzu said, "A journey of a thousand miles begins with a single step." You have taken a big first step in the process of making your portfolio by learning what a portfolio is and what it can do for you. Your reflection on this process is the most important part of your beginning, because it will shape the work you will do. Thinking about what kind of portfolio you want to create, and how it will benefit you, will propel you forward in your work. As you envision this finished product—the goal you are setting for yourself—that image will provide the impetus for you to reconstruct your ideas about what the portfolio is and can be for you. With that impetus, you will build and shape your portfolio. It will document your journey to becoming a teacher.

### What You Have Accomplished in This Chapter

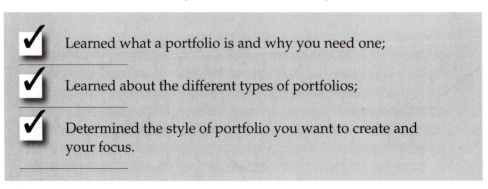

✔ Learned what a portfolio is and why you need one;

✔ Learned about the different types of portfolios;

✔ Determined the style of portfolio you want to create and your focus.

# Organizing Your Portfolio

## Checklist of Things Needed for Chapter 2

- [ ] Your "Find Your Focus" work from Chapter 1

- [ ] The standards and/or competencies used by your teacher education program

- [ ] 3- or 5-inch binder (5 inch for Developmental portfolio; 3 inch for Showcase portfolio)

- [ ] All your artifacts (e.g., lesson plans, observations, workshop notes, research papers)

- [ ] 2 sets of dividers (You will use these in Chapter 3.)

- [ ] Several packets of 3-hole-punched plastic sleeves to protect your work

## Sharpen Your Focus

How do I begin? You begin work on your portfolio by sharpening your focus and making a decision on the kind of portfolio you are making. Are you making a developmental portfolio, which will show your work from the beginning of your study to the culmination of a major stage of work such as graduating with an associate or bachelor's degree? Are you creating a showcase portfolio with only a few exemplary and comprehensive pieces of work? Are you preparing an e-portfolio? While you are a pre-service teacher, the developmental portfolio shows your progress as a developing teacher; so most professors want you to work on this kind of portfolio first. Later, after you have a major body of work from which to draw, then you can use exemplary pieces of work to develop the showcase or e-portfolio. You did this work in Chapter 1.

## Collecting Your Materials

The next step in preparing your portfolio is gathering all your pieces of work. Collect your research papers, observations, lesson plans, workshop notes, autobiographical reflections, exams, and certificates. You need to collect all the work you have done in preparation to become a teacher thus far. Even if you have just begun your first course and all you have is your first reflection on why you want to become a teacher, take it out.

You will need a 5-inch three-ring binder, two or three packs of dividers, and plastic sleeves with three holes to protect your work. In addition, get an accordion file to store materials until you place them in the portfolio itself.

In the very front inside cover of your portfolio you need identifying information to indicate that the portfolio is your property and if found, it should be returned to you. Include your name, e-mail address, and phone number for someone to contact you in case the book is lost or stolen.

## Remember Your Research—Don't Reinvent the Wheel

If you did your homework from the last chapter, you should have researched the suggested categories for organizing your portfolio according to your department by checking with professors and/or other students. That was suggested because, if your college has specific categories they require, or a particular organization of the portfolio that would help them to review and assess the portfolio, give them the organization they prefer.

You should also place a copy of the summary of the NAEYC Standards in the front of the portfolio. If your college has a set of competencies, but does not necessarily wish you to use them as your organizing sections for your portfolio, it might be a good idea to make that list of competencies an artifact in the front of the portfolio as well. You do this to show the reader that you are mindful of the standards and the competencies you are striving to achieve, and the purpose (goals and objectives) for the work. Keeping the standards and competencies in the front of the binder also keeps them available for reference as you write your reflections.

After reviewing your school's competencies, you are now more aware of objectives that are set for you in your pursuit of a degree. Because your portfolio is going to demonstrate your skills and abilities meeting these objectives, you need to create a Statement of Purpose or Portfolio Goal Statement for your portfolio. It will tell the reader what your goals and objectives are in creating this portfolio. In order to write this brief statement, reflect on why you are doing this portfolio. Consider the following questions and see whether the answers do not lead you to a Statement of Purpose.

## Reflect on Your Purpose in Creating Your Portfolio

1. Stated in your own words, what major goals or objectives do you hope to meet in your study to become a teacher? (Your program's competencies should help you identify these objectives.)

2. How will your portfolio help you to demonstrate those objectives?

3. What will the reader learn about you as a teacher based on your portfolio?

Two sample Portfolio Statements of Purpose follow. The first is a Purpose Statement for a developmental portfolio. The second is a Purpose Statement for a showcase portfolio.

---

### PORTFOLIO

#### Statement of Purpose

This developmental portfolio is a record of my work in becoming a teacher. It begins with my work at _____ Community College, and ends with my work at _____ College for my bachelor's degree. This portfolio demonstrates my abilities in observing children and recording their behavior objectively, understanding child development, and how to develop hands-on activities that help children learn. The portfolio has evidence of my lesson plans, and my abilities developing an integrated unit. It also provides evidence of my understanding of learning centers and room arrangement through my room designs, and my work adopting a play area and redesigning its materials.

You will learn through this portfolio that I am involved in the National Association for the Education of Young Children's local chapter, and have achieved certificates in First Aid, Child Abuse and Neglect, and Violence Prevention.

---

## Statement of Purpose

The purpose of this portfolio is to showcase my work as an early childhood teacher. This portfolio contains two comprehensive bodies of work, which exemplify my planning and teaching and expertise in science content, and my abilities in early childhood assessment.

The first piece of work highlighted here is an integrated unit plan on solids, liquids, and gases based on the theme of "Water," which I planned and executed with a second-grade class during my student teaching placement in P.S., in Brooklyn, New York. I have included a videotape of the science lesson, copies of student work (including science journals, and cooperative group charts of data), digital photos of the related math lesson, and my supervisor's evaluation. I have also included my self-assessment of the lesson, and my ideas for carrying out a follow-up activity.

I have included a child study that I conducted with a kindergarten child age 5 years 6 months. It is evidence of my ability to observe and record children's behavior objectively, and to assess children's development. This study was done in conjunction with my final field placement in my community college. This study includes copies of the child's work.

You will find in the professional development section, copies of my teaching certificate, and evidence of my membership in both the National Association for the Education of Young Children and the National Science Teachers Association. I have attended the NAEYC conference in NYC and several science teacher events in New York City. You will find logs and reflections on the workshops I attended at each event.

You can provide a bulleted version of the statement, which highlights the important aspects of your work and your Purpose Statement. Here is an example of a bulleted version of a Portfolio Purpose Statement.

SHOWCASE PORTFOLIO

## Statement of Purpose

The purpose of this portfolio is to showcase my work as an early childhood teacher and my expertise and interest in science education. This work demonstrates my abilities planning an integrated unit and teaching, and my knowledge of good early childhood assessment practices, and

## Statement of Purpose (con't)

presents my professional certificates. My portfolio will present the following:

- **An integrated unit plan (second grade)** on the theme of "Water"

  - videotape of the science lesson;

  - copies of student work (science journals, and cooperative learning group charts of data);

  - digital photos of the related math lesson;

  - field supervisor's evaluation;

  - self-assessment reflection on the lesson.

- **A child study** of a child age 5 years 6 months

  - objectively recorded observations;

  - a summarizing report;

  - a portfolio of the child's work.

- **Professional Certificates** including:

  - New York State Early Childhood Education teaching certificate,

  - National Association for the Education of Young Children Institute Certificate;

  - National Science Teachers Association "Life Science for Little Ones" workshops.

### Draft Your Portfolio Purpose Statement

Now that you have seen three different versions and have your own notes telling your objectives in creating the portfolio, begin to write your first draft. Think of it as telling the story of what is unique about you as a teacher as demonstrated by the work in your portfolio. How does that work demonstrate your meeting the competencies that your college or state has set? Your statement should be brief and inviting so that the reviewer wants to read through the portfolio to learn more about you.

## Table of Contents

One of the first organizing tools you will create is a Table of Contents. It will contain a list of sections, which will then be reflected in the sections in the portfolio binder. If you have not done so already, confer with a professor about the general sections they require in your department.

Speak with a student, who is further along than you and ask to see the sections he or she has created. We will create some general categories here so you can structure a Table of Contents. Using the Table of Contents, you will create a binder with the categories that are developed.

There are many divisions you can create. What you want to accomplish is to have an organization that makes sense to the reader. Two formats are presented here: one is just a general organization; and one is organized according to the NAEYC Standards. Here is a Table of Contents with a list of sections that most portfolios should have:

---

## PORTFOLIO

### Table of Contents

**Section 1. Introductory Information**

Personal Data (Name, Telephone, E-mail Address)

Portfolio Statement of Purpose

Professional Goals Statement

Resume

Autobiography

Teaching Philosophy

**Section 2. Child Development**

Observations

Child Studies

**Section 3. Curriculum and Teaching**
**(Lesson Plans, Unit Plans, Curriculum Projects)**

Play

    Dramatic Play

    Blocks

    Sand and Water

Language and Literacy

Social Studies

Science and Math

Art

Music

**Section 4. Related Specialized Coursework Projects**

Special Education

Speech and Language

Psychology

---

## PORTFOLIO

### Table of Contents (con't)

**Section 5. Research Papers**

**Section 6. Exams**

**Section 7. Professional Development**

    Certificates and Special Training

    Institutes

    Internships and Student Teaching

    Logs

    Time Sheets

The list of sections for your portfolio should serve your needs. If you have a need for a section that is not listed, create it. Nothing is written in stone in a portfolio. It is a dynamic document in that it will evolve and change. You will add sections and take others out. You will name sections and may find that you need to rename them to accommodate either new or different materials that you want to include. If you write your Table of Contents on your computer, you will easily be able to update it with the changes you make.

An alternative Table of Contents that you might wish to use is organized around the National Association for the Education of Young Children (NAEYC) Standards for Licensure, which were approved in July 2001, and the updated NAEYC policy statement, "Where We Stand on Standards for Programs to Prepare Early Childhood Professionals," published 2009. These standards were developed in connection with National Council for Accreditation of Teacher Education (NCATE) of which NAEYC is a specialty professional member.

## PORTFOLIO

### Table of Contents

- **Introductory Information**
    - Personal Data (Name, Telephone, E-mail Address)
    - Portfolio Statement of Purpose
    - Goals Statement
    - Resume
    - Autobiography
    - Teaching Philosophy

# Table of Contents (con't)

The advantage of using a Table of Contents based on the NAEYC Standards is that the organization of your work is specifically focused on the standards you are striving to attain.

### Connecting to the Standards

The new NAEYC Standards updated in 2009 have given students a lens for looking at the work they do to prepare for teaching. Excerpts from the position statement NAEYC Standards for Early Childhood Professional Preparation Programs, published 2009, used here are reprinted with the permission of the National Association for the Education of Young Children We highlighted the standards and the key elements here with some discussion of the work connected with each standard that you might include in your portfolio. You can access the entire position statement document on the NAEYC website at the following web address:

http://www.naeyc.org/files/naeyc/file/positions/ ProfPrepStandards09.pdf

If you have never read the entire document, you should because it gives not only the Standards, but a discussion of the work that you must do, and the dispositions you should hold that demonstrate your work towards the Standards You may find that work you do touches on more than one standard. In that case, if you use the standards as an organizing tool for your table of contents, you can place work into the standard section that it best fits. When you write the rationale for the piece of work, you can state that it also meets any other standard that you feel the work addresses.

**Standard 1. Promoting Child Development and Learning** speaks about your understanding of the theories and practices connected with how children grow and learn.

---

# Standards Summary

## Standard 1. Promoting Child Development and Learning

Students prepared in early childhood degree programs are grounded in a child development knowledge base. They use their understanding of young children's characteristics and needs and of the multiple interacting influences on children's development and learning to create environments that are healthy, respectful, supportive, and challenging for each child.

## Key elements of Standard 1

**1a:** Knowing and understanding young children's characteristics and needs

**1b:** Knowing and understanding the multiple influences on development and learning

**1c:** Using developmental knowledge to create healthy, respectful, supportive, and challenging learning environments

---

Your work should demonstrate your understanding of the development of the whole child including their physical, intellectual, emotional, social, and linguistic development. Your work, which helps you to understand the development of the child in the context of the familial and cultural influences on his or her development, would support your meeting this standard. Any work you have done that demonstrates your understanding of how to create and maintain a healthy learning environment and the importance of play in the lives of children will also be supportive of this standard. Projects and research papers on theories and theorists that help you to understand the development of the child including his or her unique talents and abilities, will address this standard. Work that helps you to understand any learning disabilities children may present with, and how to create an environment that supports and challenges the learning of each child, would all fall into this standard.

**Standard 2. Building Family and Community Relationships** centers on the work that you do to understand the role families play in the development of children. It includes the work you do as a teacher to strengthen your relationships with the family and make it a true partnership that supports the child.

---

## Standard 2. Building Family and Community Relationships

Students prepared in early childhood degree programs understand that successful early childhood education depends upon partnerships with children's families and communities. They know about, understand, and value the importance and complex characteristics of children's families and communities. They use this understanding to create respectful, reciprocal relationships that support and empower families and to involve all families in their children's development and learning.

## Key elements of Standard 2

**2a:** Knowing about and understanding diverse family and community characteristics

**2b:** Supporting and engaging families and communities through respectful, reciprocal relationships

**2c:** Involving families and communities in their children's development and learning

---

Projects that help you to understand the role that families and communities play in supporting the development of children, and the importance of the teacher's role in developing respectful relationships, would meet this standard. As you create work, which strengthens family involvement in the education of children, it would connect with Standard 2. Your work learning about good parent–teacher communication, assisting in parent workshops, developing parent surveys, and researching community resources would support this standard.

**Standard 3. Observing, Documenting, and Assessing to Support Young Children and Families** requires that pre-service teachers demonstrate a knowledge of observing, recording, and other forms of assessment of children's behavior that is mindful of the whole child and the child's healthy development.

Your work objectively observing and recording children's behavior in anecdotal records, observational logs, engaging in child studies, and keeping a portfolio of children's work would all fit into this category. Especially for the primary grades your ability to design interview protocols and develop teacher-made tests are examples of work addressing this standard. Your work with the early childhood team sharing information on children's interests, and talents and abilities, and maintaining confidentiality of student information will show your understanding of child assessment and would support Standard 3.

**Standard 4. Using Developmentally Effective Approaches to Connect with Children and Families** relates to the teaching practices and strategies you use to support each child's growth as you work with families.

## Key elements of Standard 4

**4a:** Understanding positive relationships and supportive interactions as the foundation of their work with children

**4b:** Knowing and understanding effective strategies and tools for early education

**4c:** Using a broad repertoire of developmentally appropriate teaching/learning approaches

**4d:** Reflecting on their own practice to promote positive outcomes for each child

The work you do to help children create healthy connections with their peers and other caring adults, and how to apply that knowledge in a developmentally appropriate way, would address this standard. The work you do in the field trying out strategies, which developmentally appropriately engage children in positive interactions, helping them to be self-regulating, would fit into this category. Your reflections on this work monitoring and adjusting the strategies and approaches you take and your thinking about this work as you teach would also fall into this section.

**Standard 5. Using Content Knowledge to Build Meaningful Curriculum** relates to your knowledge and understanding about teaching the content areas in the early childhood grades. As an early childhood teacher, you are responsible for teaching curriculum in the content areas such as language and literacy, science, mathematics, social studies, art and music and movement, and demonstrating your understanding of the knowledge base and the methodologies of teaching in those areas.

## Standard 5. Using Content Knowledge to Build Meaningful Curriculum

Students prepared in early childhood degree programs use their knowledge of academic disciplines to design, implement, and evaluate experiences that promote positive development and learning for each and every young child. Students understand the importance of developmental domains and academic (or content) disciplines in an early childhood curriculum. They know the essential concepts, inquiry tools, and structure of content areas, including academic subjects, and can identify resources to deepen their understanding. Students use their own knowledge and other resources to design, implement, and evaluate meaningful, challenging curricula that promote comprehensive developmental and learning outcomes for every young child.

## Key elements of Standard 5

**5a:** Understanding content knowledge and resources in academic disciplines

**5b:** Knowing and using the central concepts, inquiry tools, and structures of content areas or academic disciplines

**5c:** Using their own knowledge, appropriate early learning standards, and other resources to design, implement, and evaluate meaningful, challenging curricula for each child

Curriculum projects, lesson plans, unit plans, and reflections on methods used in teaching, all fall into this standard. Your reports on resources used to teach these content areas would all be work that addresses this standard. Activities, lesson, and units you create must challenge children and be appropriate for development of the whole child, promoting physical, intellectual, emotional, and social development. You must be aware of a variety of ways of assessing whether students are gaining the skills and abilities, and acquiring content that you are teaching. Your assessment should demonstrate your abilities to observe, interview, collect evidence of student work, and later, create teacher-made tests. You must be knowledgeable about the variety of learning styles and handicapping conditions of the children you teach so that your lessons involve each child. You must also be aware of issues of equity so that you are inclusive of all children regardless of gender and ethnicity as you develop curriculum. Your goal should be to develop curriculum that involves and excites each and every child in your care.

**Standard 6. Becoming a Professional** speaks about your commitment to the profession by virtue of what you know and what you do. As a teacher you must know and act using ethical principles of early childhood practice with children and families. Early childhood educators very often work in teams. You need to demonstrate the ability to work with other professionals and with parents in support of the growth and development of children. As a professional, you must strive to make your growth in knowledge and practice a lifelong pursuit. The work you do to strengthen the early childhood education profession as a whole, and enhance the services provided to children and families, would also fall under this standard.

---

## Standard 6. Becoming a Professional

Students prepared in early childhood degree programs identify and conduct themselves as members of the early childhood profession. They know and use ethical guidelines and other professional standards related to early childhood practice. They are continuous, collaborative learners who demonstrate knowledgeable, reflective, and critical perspectives on their work, making informed decisions that integrate knowledge from a variety of sources. They are informed advocates for sound educational practices and policies.

## Key elements of Standard 6

**6a:** Identifying and involving oneself with the early childhood field

**6b:** Knowing about and upholding ethical standards and other professional guidelines

**6c:** Engaging in continuous, collaborative learning to inform practice

**6d:** Integrating knowledgeable, reflective, and critical perspectives on early education

**6e:** Engaging in informed advocacy for children and the profession

---

Your work on projects intended to understand the early childhood ethics guidelines on practice would demonstrate compliance with this standard. Workshops, institutes, seminars that you take to improve as a teacher would also demonstrate work connected to this standard. Also, memberships in professional organizations would address this standard. Any work you do advocating on behalf of early childhood issues would also be a work focused on this standard.

### Create Your Table of Contents

In order to create your own Table of Contents, look first at the criteria your program is using as a way of assessing your portfolio. Look also at the sample Table of Contents you obtained from your professor, classmate, or colleague. Look at the sample Table of Contents provided in this chapter. Remember that your categories may not be hard and fast. In other words you may find that some things may seem to fall into two categories. Your answers to the following questions should help you develop your Tentative Table of Contents.

1. What items are you going to include that reflect introductory information?

2. Are you going to make a general organization Table of Contents, one based on NAEYC Standards, or one based on your program?

3. List your major sections.

4. For each of your major sections, list the subsections you anticipate needing.

5. Create a list of all of your sections and subsections.

The list of sections and subsections is your Table of Contents. You may want to check it against sample ones you have collected, and against the criteria of the program you obtained to be certain that you have all areas of competency covered.

## Preparing Sections

Your next step is to create the divisions using the dividers you have and to label each one to match the major sections and subsections listed on your Table of Contents. These labels can be written lightly in pencil if you are creating a Developmental Portfolio and are developing your portfolio as you evolve. If you are fairly certain of your sections, your labels should be clear and neatly printed or printed on your computer. After labeling the major sections, create your subdivisions and label those. Create one last miscellaneous section for materials that do not fit any category in your tentative Table of Contents.

## Organizing Your Artifacts

A portfolio is a compendium of your work, so you need to collect all of your work to select the pieces you will put in your portfolio. Here is a list of the possible artifacts that you might put into the portfolio. A comprehensive list of artifacts for your developmental portfolio is in Chapter 5. This list is organized into a potential Table of Contents.

**Introductory Material**
- Personal Data Label
- Portfolio Purpose Statement
- Professional Goal Statement
- Resume
- Autobiography
- Teaching Philosophy

**Child Development**
- Research Papers
- Projects on Room Arrangement
- Research Papers on Visiting Early Childhood Classrooms
- Curriculum Workshop Notes
- Research Papers on Child Development
- Research Papers on Early Childhood Theorists
- Research Papers on Program Models

**Observing, Documenting, and Assessing**
- Observational Logs
- Child Studies
- Checklists
- Copies of Student Work

**Using Developmentally Effective Practices to Connect Children and Families**
- Lesson Plans
    - Lesson Logs and Self-evaluation
    - Examples of Children's Work
- Unit Plans
- Curriculum Webs
- Videotapes of Pre-service Teacher-led Lessons
- Digital photographs of Pre-service Teacher-led Activities
- Teacher-made Materials and Games
- Family Involvement Projects
    - Parent Surveys
    - Parent Workshop Logs
- Community Projects
    - Community Resource List
    - Community Research Paper, field notes

**Using Content Knowledge to Build Meaningful Curriculum**
- Author Studies (Children's Books)
- Annotated Bibliographies (Children's Books)
- Research Papers on Informal Education Institutions
    - (Museums and Halls of Science)

**Becoming a Professional**
- Certificates, Logs, and Time Sheets
  - First Aid
  - Child Abuse and Neglect
  - Violence Prevention
  - CDA
  - Certificates of Workshop and Institute Participation
- Internship Logs
- Field Experience Time Sheets

Each artifact needs to be protected in plastic sleeves so that it remains fresh and pristine when being handled. Also, if you preserve your work in plastic sleeves, you will not need to punch holes in them to put them into the binder.

## Concluding Remarks

In this chapter, you have reviewed the NAEYC Standards and considered how your work connects to those standards. You have also collected your work and begun to think about how to organize it. You have looked at two different organizing tools (two different Tables of Contents). The work of collecting and classifying your artifacts, and thinking about which standards you addressed while creating them, is the foundation to building your portfolio. This thinking is giving your work a beginning shape, or form. You will refine and focus your thinking in the following chapters. As you think more deeply about specific competencies, skills, and abilities gained in the work you did, you may, more easily, write your rationale statements for your artifacts. However, this beginning thinking will make the next step easier because you are taking with you the standards, and your understandings of them, as a guide or a lens through which to examine and reflect on your work.

### What You Have Accomplished in This Chapter

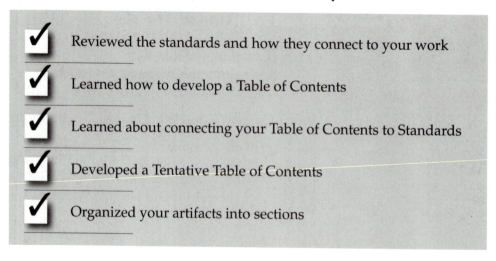

✔ Reviewed the standards and how they connect to your work

✔ Learned how to develop a Table of Contents

✔ Learned about connecting your Table of Contents to Standards

✔ Developed a Tentative Table of Contents

✔ Organized your artifacts into sections

# Reflection and Your Portfolio

In this section of the book, you will begin to explore the reflective process, and as you build your portfolio, gain an understanding of its importance to you.

By the end of Chapter 3, you will have learned a great deal about yourself, as a teacher and as a learner, and how who you are contributes to how you will teach. You will also have developed artifacts for your portfolio that result in:

- your professional goals statement;

- your autobiography;

- your philosophical teaching statement.

By the end of the Chapter 4, you will have learned how to use reflection to develop a rationale statement for different kinds of artifacts in your portfolio such as observations, child studies, and lesson and unit plans.

# First Reflections and Your Portfolio

Reflection is the act of thinking critically about practice, or what you do as a teacher. You reflect to:

- better understand what you do as a teacher;
- look closely at what your past experiences bring to your teaching;
- actively participate in your own growth.

You will find that there is a myriad of experiences that helped to form who you are and who you will become as a teaching professional. Reflection allows you to think about those experiences, sort them out, and make the connections among your experiences, your actions and their consequences. Reflection gives you an active role in shaping your own future. If you did not think in a deliberative way about what you teach, how you teach, and those experiences and influences that shape your teaching, you would be no more than a robot. A teacher has the responsibility for the care and education of young children and, therefore, must be aware and thoughtful about what she does.

As a novice teacher, you will find yourself thinking about your role as a teacher. You will begin to think about your values and beliefs and how they impact you as a teacher. Reflection is the process that engages you in that thought. Reflection is actively connecting experiences to their consequences.

Your portfolio is a documentation of your reflection on your work as a teacher. It begins with reflections on the time before you became a teacher, so that you may look at the influences that affect who you are as a teacher, and what you believe. Once you are in the field, working with children, the main body of your work will include reflection on the decisions and choices you are making as you plan, observe, and teach.

This chapter of the book is called, "First Reflections and Your Portfolio," because here you will encounter tasks that will have you examine who you are, what you think, and how that impacts you as a future teacher. Such beginning reflections are important, because they elicit your prior experiences, and help you to identify the values and assumptions you bring to teaching. Thinking about these values and assumptions, and learning from them is one of the first steps to professional development. Sometimes the things we value, and the assumptions we make, influence us on an unconscious level. You must strive to be conscious and thoughtful about your actions. You are entrusted with the care of young children and cannot afford to react without thinking.

In this chapter, you are asked to reflect on your own experiences as a young child in a family, and the beliefs that you adopted during that period of your life. You may want to reflect upon your school experiences that influenced you, and the beliefs and assumptions you hold today, as a result of those experiences. You may also want to look at community and cultural influences upon your ideas about education. These first reflections will give you a sense of the experiences that were significant to you, and how they began to form your ideas about teaching and learning. Experiences are powerful motivations for the choices you will make as a teacher. As you reflect upon your experiences, you will find that they can be greater motivating factors for the way you teach than are the theories that you read. As Stephen Brookfield, an expert in reflective practice, puts it:

> Analyzing our autobiographies as learners has important implications for how we teach. Our experiences as learners are felt at a visceral, emotional level that is much deeper than that of reason. The insights and meanings for teaching that we draw from these deep experiences are likely to have a profound and long-lasting influence. They certainly affect us more powerfully than methods or injunctions that we learn from textbooks or hear from superiors.
>
> (Brookfield, p. 31)

Given the profound and long-lasting effects that these experiences can have, you must treat your early experiences with respect and learn as much as you can about the implications they have for you as a teacher.

## Constructing Your Professional Goals Statement

Your Professional Goals statement is one of the first documents a reader will see. It must, therefore, state your goals clearly, succinctly, and professionally. From your vantage point, writing a goals statement gives you the opportunity to formulate your thoughts about your career goals and objectives. The reader of your portfolio needs to know what your intentions are with as much specificity as you can give at the time. We said earlier that a portfolio is a dynamic, growing, changing document. It will grow and change as you, your hopes and desires grow and change. Over time, your goals will change, but right now, you must assess what is it that you aspire to in a career in early childhood education.

In preparation to write your goals statement you will do some reflection and some research. First reflect on your goals using the following questions as a guide.

### Reflection 1: A Career in Early Childhood Education

1. What is your career goal in the field of early childhood education?

2. Do you want to become a professional who serves children and families, but not necessarily a teacher (e.g., school social worker, psychologist, school administrator, or guidance counselor)?

3. Why do you want to be an early childhood teacher or professional? Give at least three reasons.

4. What experience do you have, if any, working with young children?

5. What attributes do you bring to teaching?

6. What questions or concerns, if any, do you have about making a career in this field?

7. What steps are you planning to take in your education to become an early childhood professional?

## Doing Your Homework

Major life decisions such as becoming a teacher should be done with as much information as you can gather. You may want to interview people who have chosen the career path in which you are interested. You may wish to visit and observe early childhood settings to find out whether the field is truly for you. You should visit at least two settings. You may wish to visit a public or private preschool, a Head Start, or a primary grade in a public or private school. Here are a few things to think about when you visit.

## Reflection 2: Visit to Preschool, Kindergarten, or Primary Grade

1. What is the setting (public/private, childcare, Head Start, pre-kindergarten, primary grades, public school, private school)?

2. What is the age group(s)?

3. What is the adult-child ratio?

4. How is the room arranged? Sketch the floor plan.

5. What kind of activities are you seeing (whole class instruction, small group instruction, choice time)?

6. If you can tell, what is the teaching philosophy or approach of the teacher (child-centered, teacher-directed, eclectic)?

7. What is the daily schedule?

8. How do the children react to what is happening (actively engaged, challenged, interested, bored, frustrated)?

9. How do you feel about being in this classroom?

10. Is this a grade and setting in which you would like to teach? Why? Why not?

## Interview a Professional in the Field

Sometimes you may have the opportunity to interview an early childhood professional to learn about the joys and the challenges of the work. It is important to choose people who enjoy working with children and families and who will give you honest feedback. People who may be burned out are not good choices, because they may have forgotten what drew them to the profession. You should also try and look for people who are working in settings that are fulfilling. Here are some sample questions.

## Sample Interview Questions

1. What do you most enjoy about this work?

2. What do you dislike about this work?

3. What do you do in a given day?

4. How does your work impact children and families?

5. What characteristics, talents, and abilities do you feel you bring to this work?

Here are two Sample Goals Statements, which should give you an idea of how to craft your Professional Goals statement that will give the reader a sense of your career interests and direction.

---

### SAMPLE PROFESSIONAL GOALS STATEMENTS

I am an undergraduate student currently finishing my course work in early childhood education. My ultimate career goal is to teach in a public school as a science cluster teacher. I was exposed to this field opportunity when I visited a public school in my research on early childhood settings. I saw a teacher teach a lesson on worms to second graders, and I was "hooked." I have a major in early childhood and a minor in science. I have taken the course in science education in college. I think teaching science to young children will develop in them the love of science that I have.

I intend to pursue my masters in science education at _____ College. I volunteer at the Hall of Science, and, I would love to create science programs for children to help them see science all around them.

---

My immediate goal is to become an early childhood teacher working in the Head Start Program. I want to gain experience working with children and families because my ultimate goal is to get my bachelor degree and then my masters and to become a social worker. I would like to help families, especially immigrant families, learn about the resources available to them.

---

## Draft Your Goals Statement

Based on your reflection on a career in early childhood education, any visits you have done to find out about actual settings, as well as any other research you may have done by asking questions of professors and teachers you know, you should write a first draft of a goals statement. Later, as you revise it, especially if you want to use it for a capstone portfolio for a particular employer or graduate school, you may wish to tweak it and sharpen the focus, but for now, write out your early childhood education goals.

## Constructing Your Autobiography

One of the important documents in your portfolio is your autobiography. Your autobiography tells the story of who you are and what shaped your desire to become a teacher. Your autobiography is made up of the significant events and influences in your life. Typically, people are shaped by the institutions, which influence them. Your family, your schools and teachers, your community and culture, all may have had a role in shaping who you are today. The institutions that were responsible for your education and shaping your beginning ideas about education, play a big role in helping you to define yourself as a teacher. The things you value, and the assumptions you make about what a good teacher is, and should do, were influenced by the institutions that shaped your early education.

Begin constructing your autobiography by reflecting on your early experiences of family and school. Do some reflective writing in answer to the following questions in the next section.

### Reflection 3: Memories of My Family, My Schools, My Community and Me

The family is the first constellation of people who influence us and shape who we are.

1. Describe your earliest memories of growing up in your family.

2. Do you remember events, which were significant for you, as a young child that happened when you were growing up with parent(s), sibling(s), grandparent(s), friend(s)?

3. Have your memories of family influenced who you are today, and your desire to become a teacher?

4. What are your early memories of school?

5. What are your memories of good teachers?

6. What were the attributes of good teachers? Poor teachers?

7. What are your memories of good supportive schools?

8. What attributes do you have that will contribute to your becoming a good teacher?

9. What, if any, influence did your community and culture(s) have in your desire to become a teacher?

## Reflection 4: Writing Your Autobiography

Based on the reflection you did on A Career in Early Childhood Education and your reflections on self, family, and school, write a first draft of your autobiography.

Here are some guiding questions:

1. How would you introduce yourself? Where are you now in your preparation as a teacher?

2. Why do you want to be a teacher?

3. What significant event(s) took you in this direction?

4. What early influences shaped you, and contributed to who you are today?

5. Were there any teachers or school experiences that influenced you and your desire to become a teacher?

6. What special talents, abilities, or other personal attributes, do you bring to teaching?

7. What traits in your character and belief system do you bring to teaching?

8. Besides teaching do you have any other goals in life?

---

### SAMPLE AUTOBIOGRAPHICAL STATEMENT

I have wanted to become a teacher for as long as I can remember, but I remember making a conscious choice to do so in the fourth grade. I had a wonderful teacher, whose name was Ms. Klein. She had a sparkle in her eye, and always had interesting projects for us to do and ways for us to be creative. She encouraged a love for reading by having us select books from the class library and read at our own pace. We also wrote in our journals about what we liked about passages in the book, and characters we read about.

I am currently finishing my student teaching at _____ College, and completing the teaching certification process in early childhood education. I expect to graduate in June of 201_.

As I look back, I can see that my parents and grandparents played a big role in my wanting to get an education, and to become a teacher. My parents were born in the West Indies and they worked very hard to send my brother and me to school. My parents always found out about the best educational programs for us. I was in the gifted class, because my mother found out about the testing program. I took part in a Saturday class at the museum because my dad found out about it. On Sundays, whenever I needed him to do so, my dad would drive me to the library to do work for my school projects.

The value I think I will bring to teaching is a love for learning, which I got from my parents and my teachers. I want to pass that love for learning on to children. I believe that if children are excited about learning, they will be motivated to make education a big part of their lives. I think I also bring perseverance. I always stick to something until I finish it. That was something my grandmother taught me. "Never give up," she would say. In my field placement, a cooperating teacher said to me, "I notice that when you feel a child does not understand, you try to teach the concept another way the next day." I think perseverance is a trait that will help me to meet the needs of all of the children in my class. I also want to teach children to have that same ability, so that they will accomplish their goals.

My immediate goal is to be an early childhood teacher. I hope to continue my education and get my master's degree in guidance. Down the road, I hope to be a guidance counselor. I want to instill a love for learning and help children solve any personal problems they may have, so that they can move ahead in their education. I also want to be able to guide children to get into programs in middle school that will help them go to college.

## Constructing Your Teaching Philosophy

Finally, you will reflect upon your developing philosophy of education. This early reflection will grow into a philosophical statement at the culmination of each significant step in your educational career. You may write one at the end of a two-year associate degree, or a four-year college degree, as you seek licensure, and again as you seek entrance to graduate school. Your philosophy will be enriched by your experience and further education throughout your life.

In order to begin writing your philosophical statement, look back at your visits to early childhood education centers. They should bring the text materials on the theoretical foundations of education, child development theory, and the models of early childhood education to life. These visits should give you a sense of the kind of classroom environment you hope to create for children. Reflect on your field experiences, and think about the methods you observed that you hope to incorporate into your teaching. What methods have you tried, and hope to continue using, as a teacher?

Look back at your reflection, "Memories of My Family, My Schools, My Community and Me" and on the teachers and their attributes that you hope to incorporate into your teaching. Think about the qualities of good teaching that you thought you might like to emulate.

Look back on your class work in early childhood and your readings of the theories and those philosophical ideas about early childhood education that resonated for you. When you were engaged in curriculum class work, what methodologies seemed to be those that you would adopt? Use the following reflection questions as a guide for exploring your own philosophical ideas, including your values and principles, about child development, teaching, and learning that you hold dear. These will come together in your Teaching Philosophical Statement.

### Reflection 5: My Teaching Philosophy

1. From your experience, what are the characteristics of a good teacher?

2. What are the characteristics of your ideal early childhood classroom?

3. From what you have learned, are there any theories or approaches that you have adopted as part of your teaching philosophy?

4. What do you value as a teacher?

5. What principles do you hold for yourself as a teacher?

6. Are there any theories or practices you wish to learn more about?

### Writing Your Teaching Philosophy

After you have reflected on the previous questions, you can use those notes to compose your first draft of your Teaching Philosophy. If you are working on the computer, you can simply cut and paste from your notes.

Here is a sample teaching philosophy statement of a student who is graduating from a community college.

---

#### MY TEACHING PHILOSOPHY

I have developed my teaching philosophy from the many good teachers who I have had, and the good theories about teaching, which I have read about and seen in practice. I believe that all children can learn, and it is our job as teachers to make school exciting and interesting. I believe in child-centered learning, and that children learn best in hands-on activities. I believe that children are different from each other, and learn at their own pace, and that we as teachers must try to meet each child's needs.

I believe that parents should be involved in their children's education. I have seen, and taken part in, parent workshops in the Head Start Center where I interned, and I have seen how much parents want to know about what their children are learning, and how they can help them.

---

My ideal classroom would be a kindergarten or first-grade class in a public school, because I believe in public school education. It would have centers for children to explore, with challenging activities that help them learn to read and write and do math. I would teach as much as possible in small groups so that I would know that all children are learning.

I have just begun learning about balanced literacy and the writing process, and how to help children write using journals. The public school in which I am doing a field experience has this program. I hope to learn more about that. I expect to attend the NAEYC conference in my area this year, and I want to focus on workshops in writing and reading.

Your first draft of this statement should be revised over time. You will find that new methodologies and theories that resonate for you will appear in this document. Your growing experience will add conviction to your principles and you may add new ones, or frame the ones you already have in a slightly different way. You will find that the process of reflection done to help you to unearth the principles and values that guide you will be the same. You will be able to use these reflective questions in the future, should you need to add to your teaching philosophy.

## Concluding Remarks

In this chapter, you have done the work of crystallizing your thoughts about who you are as a beginning teacher, and what you think about teaching and learning. By drafting your Autobiography, and your Teaching Philosophical Statement, you are doing this work as well. Who you are and what you believe, and the values and principles you hold, gives your portfolio a direction. This direction is driven by your thoughts and beliefs. You have also crafted your Professional Goals Statement, which will, when finalized, tell the reader where you are headed in your career. These three important documents give your portfolio a sense of purpose, which is clearly fixed on your future as a teacher. Even though these documents are currently in draft form, they preview the story you are beginning to develop of yourself as a teacher, which will be presented as your portfolio.

## What You Have Accomplished in This Chapter

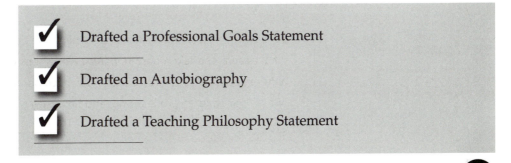

✔ Drafted a Professional Goals Statement

✔ Drafted an Autobiography

✔ Drafted a Teaching Philosophy Statement

# Reflections on Your Work

## Checklist of Things Needed for Chapter 4

☐ Your Introductory Material (Table of Contents, Professional Goals Statement, Portfolio Statement of Purpose, Autobiography, Teaching Philosophy)

☐ The standards and/or competencies used by your teacher education program

☐ All your artifacts (e.g., lesson plans, observations, workshop notes, research papers) organized into the sections of your Table of Contents

In an earlier chapter it was stated that a portfolio is not a scrapbook. A scrapbook is just a collection of things. Reflection is what makes your collection of work into a portfolio, because the reflection that you do about your work tells the reader about you as a professional. The process of reflection binds the work together into a story about you as a teacher. Your reflection explains how you see your work. It tells about your analysis and evaluation of your work. It tells what you have learned by virtue of that work. Finally, it tells how you would improve upon your work.

Reflection is the process that engages you in critical thought. Reflection is actively connecting experiences to their consequences. John Dewey (1944) described reflection this way:

> Thought or reflection . . . is the discernment of the relation between what we try to do and what happens in consequence . . . Thinking [reflection] is the accurate and deliberate instituting of connections between what is done and its consequences.
>
> (Dewey, pp. 144, 151)

As you reflect on both your past experiences and your work, and you see the connections of both to what you now do, you can make thoughtful decisions about what you will do in the future. This active reflection (or thinking) and decision making, helps you grow as a professional. The process begins again as you add to your experience and reflect once more.

As a novice teacher, you will find yourself reflecting on what you do while you are working. Schon (1987) called that "reflection-in-action": "It is that process that allows us to reshape what we are working on, *while* we are working on it." You will also reflect on what you have learned from the lessons you have taught, or the units you planned and implemented, and the observations you have conducted. These reflections, *after* there have been lessons learned by you, are what Schon calls "reflection-on-action." All of these reflections will engage you in thinking about the work that you are doing, and how the values, assumptions, and beliefs that you bring to the work, impact your teaching. Each time you experience something new, and reflect upon it, it will bring you to a new place in your thinking. Reflection will help you to actively grow and develop into the teacher you hope and strive to be.

Your portfolio will give you the opportunity to reveal your thinking about your work. This is important to you as a teacher, because it helps you to crystallize your thoughts about teaching and learning. It also allows you to think about the theories and philosophical ideas that you are learning about and connect them to your practice. It allows you to learn about your thinking so that you can grow.

It helps you crystallize your thoughts, because in order to write down your thoughts, you must think them through and truly understand them (metacognition). It allows you to step back from practice, and understand the connections to the theories and philosophies about which you are learning. Making those connections deepens your understandings of what you know. Depth of understanding can strengthen your conviction about why you are engaging in a particular practice. You grow, as you better understand what you do, because you then have a greater understanding of your methods and your knowledge base.

You will find that you use reflection throughout the process as you construct your portfolio. You use reflection as you select the artifacts that you will include. You use reflection as you try to decide how a particular piece of work helps you to meet the standards or competencies that your college or program requires. You are also using reflection when you articulate the rationale for including a piece of work to represent you as a developing professional.

## Selecting Artifacts of Your Work

As you look at the work you have done to become a teacher, you must select pieces of work to fit the purpose of the portfolio you are creating. You should also be thinking about the audience who will be scrutinizing the portfolio, and what they want to know about you. If you are doing a developmental portfolio, you must provide material from the beginning of your journey to become a teacher to the current time. This will be a chronological presentation of material. However, even within the entire body of work, you may be selective. You may want to show only your best work. For example, if you did a rough draft of a research paper for feedback, and got feedback on how to improve it, you might show only the final version of that work, with its incorporated changes. Later research papers you include in the portfolio will demonstrate your further growth and development as a researcher.

You may want to select artifacts that demonstrate the development of different aspects of your teaching. You may want to select pieces of work that demonstrate your skills as an observer and recorder of children's behavior. You may wish to demonstrate your ability to plan and execute lessons. You also may wish to select artifacts that show your knowledge of issues, such as family or community involvement, diversity, or special education.

Thinking about yourself as a teacher and deciding on the abilities you wish to portray is another important aspect of reflection on your work. In essence, you are asking yourself, "Who am I as a teacher, and who am I striving to become?" As you engage in this kind of thought you are really reflecting about the kind of professional you are, and who you are choosing to be in the future. As you select work to be presented, you are choosing the aspects of your ability that you feel are essential to being an early childhood professional.

If you are preparing a showcase or e-portfolio, you will wish to select exemplary work. Because the showcase and the e-portfolio are likely to be viewed by readers who have less time to peruse a large body of work, you should also select a small collection of pieces that highlight the teaching abilities sought by the reader. For example, if you are providing material to a principal in a public school, you may wish to demonstrate a breadth of experience with, and knowledge of, children in pre-kindergarten through grade three. You will want to show knowledge of content in curriculum for those grades. If, on the other hand, you are applying for a job at a Head Start center, you may wish to select artifacts that focus on your knowledge of four year olds, and the issues of family and community involvement. In essence, you should create a selection of artifacts geared to the work, or educational goals you have. You will want to select a group of artifacts that tell a story about you as a teacher.

Particularly in the e-portfolio, you may want to be mindful of the visual nature of the artifacts that you select, and the story you wish to tell. Given that your materials will be shown on a computer screen, they should be prepared for the reader so that the reader focuses on the aspects of your abilities that you are portraying. (Examples of this preparation appear later in this chapter and in the chapter on e-Portfolios.)

## What? So What? Now What? An Easy Rationale Test

As you think about selecting an artifact for your portfolio, you should apply a simple test to it. This test will help you write the rationale statement that accompanies the artifact. The rationale statement tells what the artifact is and why you are including it. You can employ a commonly used strategy for writing a reflection based on the thinking of many theorists and researchers in reflective practice referred to as, "What? So What? Now What?" This strategy will focus you on describing your work, analyzing and understanding what it means for you as a teacher, and thinking about how you will apply it in the future.

When you first look at an artifact you need to be able to describe it for the reader.

What is it? What work did you do as a teacher to develop it? For example, if you have an artifact that is a unit, it is helpful to the reader if you describe what they will see. For example, "This artifact is an integrated unit I planned on the theme of "Bears" for kindergarteners. It contains science, math, and art lessons, with pictures of children's artwork."

The second question you should ask yourself has to do with the phrase, "So What?" This question relates to why this artifact is here. What did you learn that is evidenced in this artifact? What does it show about your growth? What understandings did you gain? For example, "In the science lesson, I helped children use the science process skills of observation and measurement. In doing this math lesson, I learned how to create a picture recipe chart for making oatmeal. The children were able to 'read' the chart, and make individual bowls of oatmeal. My art lesson engaged the children in a sequencing activity."

"Now what?" This question relates to what new goals are you setting for yourself, based on this experience? How does this artifact demonstrate a turning point, or stepping-stone to more growth? How do you plan to use this experience and knowledge in the future? For example, this integrated unit taught me the importance of planning using themes.

As you analyze each artifact, test it using this easy-to-apply Rationale Test, by answering these three questions:

1. What is this artifact and what did you do to develop it? (What?)

2. How does this artifact demonstrate my growth as a professional and help me meet the Standards? (So What?)

3. How will I use what I have learned in the future? (Now What?)

You will find that as you test some artifacts using these questions some artifacts will seem to represent you and your growth better than others. You may find that as you look at an artifact, you are able to articulate how the work done on it helps you to meet the criteria your program, college, or the state sets for you as a standard for licensure. If an artifact satisfies the test by exemplifying something important about you as a teacher, shows your professional growth, helps you to meet the standards of your program, college, or state licensing agency, and represents abilities you will use in your future career, it is probably a good choice.

Here is an example of how you would apply the answers to the previous questions to an artifact.

This is an example of a community college student, who is finishing her second year of study, and has conducted a child study of a boy who is four years and two months old. The study consists of five observations during different activities in the child's day, on different days. There is, at the end of the study, a summarizing report on her findings, and a statement of what she has learned. Her observations are graded using check minus, check, or check plus. The first two observations received check minus grades, and comments about the need to be more descriptive and objective. Judgmental and labeling statements were circled. The last three observations were exemplary. She met with her professor to talk about the differences between objective and subjective comments. The student was invited by the teacher to attend a parent–teacher conference. She was not allowed to comment, but she could listen. She then consulted with the cooperating teacher and included her notes on this meeting in her final report. In that final paper, the student was able to identify the turning point, in which she learned about being more objective, and to articulate how her observations related to what she learned earlier about child development.

Here is an example of a test done by that two-year student who used this test against her child study observational logs.

**1. What is this artifact and what did you do to develop it? (What?)**

These are observation logs and they show my abilities to observe and record children's behavior objectively.

**2. How does this artifact demonstrate my growth as a professional and help me meet the Standards? (So What?)**

It shows that I have improved in my ability to become more detailed in my observation. I am now much more objective. I am more aware of what the goals of observation are to describe behavior without judgments. I no longer label children. It shows that I learn from my mistakes. It shows I can collaborate with my colleagues, my cooperating teacher, and a parent. It shows that I can learn from them, which adds to my work. This work helped me to understand how to be responsible in my assessment of children by not bringing my old values of what was good or bad behavior to my observing and labeling a child. I use observation to understand the child and how to improve what I do in the classroom. This artifact also shows what I learned about the importance of learning from parents about their children, and working with them in a partnership.

NAEYC Standard 3 Observing, Documenting, and Assessing to Support Young Children and Families, 3a: Understanding the goals, benefits, and uses of assessment 3b: Knowing about assessment partnerships with families and with professional colleagues 3c: Knowing about and using observation, documentation, and other appropriate assessment tools and approaches 3d: Understanding and practicing responsible assessment to promote positive outcomes for each child.

**3. How will I use what I have learned in the future? (Now What?)**

I look at children differently. I observe to learn, not to judge. I understand what it means to be objective in assessing children's behavior by simply recording what they do and say. If I take the time to observe one child, I can learn about him, other children, and my program. I will take the time to observe when I teach, to learn more about my students, and how to improve my teaching.

## Using Standards as Your Guide: NAEYC or INTASC

As you test each artifact, using the criteria of the three questions put forth previously, you will note that the standards are an excellent guide for determining whether you should include a particular artifact. You will notice in the previous exercise that the NAEYC Standards that the student refers to in answering the question, "How does this artifact demonstrate my growth as a professional and help me meet the standards?" relate directly to why this artifact is a good choice. Here, you have an artifact that demonstrates the student's abilities in observing and recording, as well as an understanding of the goals of assessment. It also shows that she is practicing responsible assessment, while knowing about assessment partnerships, and understanding child development. These skills are cited in the standards because they indicate the abilities that the profession expects of early childhood teachers. Artifacts that demonstrate these developing abilities are perfect for your portfolio because they show that you are developing into someone who can use assessment methods appropriate to young children and can understand the development of young children.

Although the NAEYC Standards have been cited as a reference for judging the value of your answers to the previous test, this test can be used to select an artifact based on the particular standards of your college or university. Some colleges and universities use the Interstate New Teacher Assessment Support Consortium or INTASC Standards. INTASC Standards can be found at the website of the Council of Chief State School Officers.

http://www.ccsso.org/Resources/Programs/Interstate_Teacher_ Assessment_Consortium_(INTASC).html.

Any standards that your college or university prefer should be used to test an artifact for inclusion. The competencies listed in the syllabi of your courses are also standards by which you are being judged. As you look at artifacts, hold them up to the standards and competencies that you are trying to achieve. If they seem to move you closer to reaching that standard, then it may well be a good choice for your portfolio.

You can and should discuss with your professors, and with your peers, how your artifacts support your growth according to the standards of your program. Your professors set goals for your development and, as you discuss certain artifacts, they may see a need for an artifact that expresses your ability to reach a standard that you have overlooked. A fellow student may have an idea about valuable artifacts based on courses she has taken, and the criteria that have been pointed out to her. As you look critically at artifacts and test them against the standards, you will become more familiar with the standards and how they guide not only the selection of artifacts, but also your growth as a professional.

Test a few of the artifacts you've selected for inclusion in your portfolio using the Easy Rationale Test that follows.

### EASY RATIONALE TEST

1. What is the artifact and what did you do to develop it? (What?)

2. How does this artifact demonstrate my growth as a professional and help me meet the Standards? (So What?)

3. How will I use what I have learned in the future? (Now What?)

A rationale statement accompanies an artifact in your portfolio, and tells the reader why that particular artifact has been included. It was stated earlier in this chapter that reflection helps you to sharpen and crystallize your ideas about teaching and learning, and will give you the opportunity to reveal your thinking about your work. Writing a rationale is the opportunity you have to share your thinking about why an artifact was important to include in your portfolio, and important to your growth as a teacher. It is a chance to reveal your ability to assess your own growth. Reflecting in a rationale statement shows that you are aware of the skills and abilities teachers need to have if they are to be contributing and knowledgeable professionals.

As you are writing a rationale, you should be aware of the kind of portfolio you are preparing and the audience it will meet. For example, if you are creating a developmental portfolio, your audience may be your professors, and a potential employer. You may want to be sure that your rationale demonstrates your understanding of theory and how it plays out in practice. The rationale along with the actual work, gives you an added opportunity to share your thinking about the profession.

If you are creating a showcase portfolio, you may wish to demonstrate your ability to understand the practice and underlying theory, as well as the complexity of teaching. In other words, you may wish to articulate the broader implications of what you have learned. Once you are at the stage of producing a showcase or summative portfolio, the reader is expecting that you have arrived at some broad understandings about teaching and learning that relate to the profession at large. In other words, in your developmental portfolio you may have been focused on yourself and your individual skills, and how you would use them in the future. In a showcase portfolio, you should be looking back on that experience and saying, "I learned not only about myself, but about teaching, and children, and the profession."

If you are doing an e-portfolio, you may wish to add another consideration toward making sure that you show your broad understanding, while keeping the presentation sharp and focused, and visually appealing. The e-Portfolio is presented in a visual media, and so you have to sculpt your rationale to fit that media. How does one write each of these kinds of rationales? Let's take them one at a time.

The answers to the three-question test for each artifact contain most of your rationale statement. Take the case of the student who tested her logs in the earlier task. If she were to write a rationale, she could use much of what she has already written in the three-rationale test.

# Rationale on Child Development and Observing

## RATIONALE STATEMENT

This child study was conducted during my second year of coursework at _____ Community College, when I was placed at _____ Head Start Center. These logs show my ability to observe and record children's behavior objectively, and my growth in this ability during the seven weeks of this project. It shows that I have improved in my ability to write more detailed observations. I am now much more objective in my recording. I am more aware of how to describe behavior without judgments and labeling. This child study was an opportunity for me to learn from my cooperating teacher, my classmates in seminar, my professor, and most of all, from the child I was observing, and his parent. I learned that if you observe closely and objectively, over a period of time, you will gain a better understanding of a child, and of the development of all children.

This study was particularly interesting to me because I noticed how the child started activities and did not finish them. I had remembered thinking about wanting to label this behavior, and not doing so. As I reflected on my recording, I recognized this behavior as being in Erickson's stage of Initiative vs. Guilt. This observation in particular showed me that children in this stage tend to want to get into things, but do not have the ability to stay with an activity. It was so interesting to see the theory that we learned, come to life in a real child. This knowledge helps me be more supportive and understanding of four year olds in routines such as clean up, and as they learn to enjoy sticking with an activity until they finish it.

This project shows my work addressing NAEYC Standard 1, Promoting Child Development and Learning, because of how much I learned about how child development theory, and how children develop psycho-socially. It also addresses Standard 3, Observing, Documenting, and Assessing to Support Young Children and Families because I have learned a great deal about observation and recording children's behavior objectively and keeping detailed anecdotal records to learn about a child. I learned about responsible assessment, and working collaboratively with colleagues and parents to use assessment to support children's development.

The Developmental Portfolio statement is written in a narrative. It utilizes the answers to the questions in the three-question test. Next is a sample rationale statement for a Showcase or e-Portfolio. This rationale statement is written using a bulleted style and highlights aspects of the student's work for the reader. This is especially important in the Showcase Portfolio because you are highlighting your best work and you want it to stand out. It is important in an e-portfolio also because the rationale will be viewed on a computer screen and you want information to stand out on the screen.

## SHOWCASE PORTFOLIO

### Rationale Statement

I have included five observations of a child study that was conducted during a field placement at _____ Head Start Center in my second year of study at _____ Community College. This child study shows my ability:

- to observe and record children's behavior objectively;

- to become more detailed in my observations;

- to grow in my understanding of principles of responsible assessment;

- to grow as a professional.

**How This Project Changed Me**

At the beginning of the child study, I did not understand the meaning of objective observing. I used judgmental language and labeling. By midway I improved greatly, and I am now more aware of what the goals of observation are: to describe behavior objectively; to describe what a child does and says without judgments and labeling. This child study was an opportunity for me to learn from my cooperating teacher, my classmates in seminar, my professor, and most of all, the child I was observing. I learned that if you observe closely, objectively, and over a period of time, you will gain a better understanding of a child.

**Connecting Theory and Practice**

This project also helped me to observe child development theory in practice by observing the way the child started activities and did not necessarily want to finish them and demonstrating that he was in Erickson's stage of Initiative vs. Guilt. I realized that through observation you can learn about the development of the child you are observing and about the development of all children.

## Rationale Statement

My understanding of how children develop during this stage of Erickson's Initiative, and the later stage, Industry, taught me a great deal about why teachers must be understanding of four year olds, their stage of development, and how teachers in the program can support them in learning to enjoy finishing activities by praising their efforts.

**The Standards**

This project demonstrates my work addressing the NAEYC Standard 1, Promoting Child Development and Learning, because of how much I learned about how child development theory related to my observations of this child. This project shows my progress in reaching Standard 3 because I learned a great deal about observation and recording children's behavior objectively. I learned how to responsibly assess and avoid labeling, and how to work collaboratively with colleagues to use assessment to support children. I consulted with my cooperating teacher and gathered information from the child's parent for this child study, and learned the value of this collaboration.

The Showcase Rationale is bulleted and has sections so that the reader is focused on the specific topics without having to read the whole narrative.

The Sample Rationale Statement for the e-Portfolio needs to convey information about you as a teacher and why the artifact is included, but it must do so in concise, focused bullets, without a great deal of narrative. You will need to consider also, that it will need to be conveyed visually on a computer screen, so the information has to have less narrative, but still tell the story of the student's growth in this project.

## E-PORTFOLIO

## Reflections on a Child Study

Here are three logs of a child study I conducted at _____ Head Start.

My subject was a boy who was 4 years 2 months of age.

When doing this study, I was permitted to observe the child at play, during transitions, and outdoors, and sit in on a parent teacher conference.

This study shows my abilities to:

- to observe and record children's behavior objectively;

- to grow in my understanding of responsible assessment;

- to connect child development theory to practice;

- to work as part of an early childhood team.

⇨ /▢ ⇦

**Example of an e-Portfolio Rationale Statement**

**The three logs show my progress from having little understanding of objective observation to writing logs with exemplary ratings showing growth in:**

— objective observing and well written recording;

— understanding the goals of responsible assessment and applying them:

— applying child development theory to my analysis of children's behavior.

This work addresses NAEYC Standards 1, 3a, 3b, 3c and 3d.

**Upload and link to three logs here.**

**Example of e-Portfolio Reflection on a Child Study with reference to the Standards and a place to link to your uploaded logs.**

Example of e-Portfolio Reflection on a Child Study continued.

Example of e-Portfolio Reflection on a Child Study completed.

## Rationale on Lessons and Unit Plans

When writing a rationale for a lesson plan, you can follow the same process as selecting an artifact. Look at the lessons and units that you have prepared, and ask the same three questions:

1. What is this artifact and what did you do to develop it? (What?)

2. How does this artifact demonstrate my growth as a professional and help me meet the Standards? (So What?)

3. How will I use what I have learned in the future? (Now What?)

The following example is of a student who has done a three-lesson unit plan for a science and math methods course.

A fourth-year student developed a unit around the topic of Oobleck, making Oobleck with a group of second graders. Her artifacts consist of a science and math lesson plan for making the Oobleck, a language and literacy lesson charting the characteristics of solids and liquids, and a creative writing activity wherein the children wrote stories about living in a land of Oobleck, and her description and evaluation of the lessons. She included the chart, comparing solids and liquids, which the children dictated, and stories they wrote about living in a land of Oobleck, as evidences of student work.

Here is the test of her artifacts with the three-question test to see whether it is an appropriate set of artifacts for her portfolio.

## EASY RATIONAL TEST

### 1. What is this artifact and what did you do to develop it? (What?)

This is an integrated unit, including a science, math, and language arts and literacy lesson for second graders. I planned, implemented, and evaluated the lesson, and have collected my students' charts and stories.

### 2. How does this artifact demonstrate my growth as a professional and help me meet the Standards? (So What?)

This artifact shows my growth through the analysis and evaluation of the lesson, my suggestions for follow up, my knowledge of science and math content, and my understanding of the methodology of teaching science and math using a hands-on approach, and cooperative learning groups. NAEYC Standard 4. Using Developmentally Effective Approaches to Connect Children and Families. 4b: Knowing and understanding effective strategies and tools for early education. Standard 5. Using Content Knowledge to Build Meaningful Curriculum.

### 3. How will I use what I have learned in the future? (Now What?)

I will use my understanding of how to manage cooperative learning groups by being sure the group has tasks to do so that they are focused. I will, whenever I can, plan integrated units, because I learned that each lesson builds on the other. I will always make hands-on science an integral part of my planning, because children love it.

## SAMPLE RATIONALE ON LESSON PLANS AND UNIT FOR DEVELOPMENTAL PORTFOLIO

Here I have presented an integrated unit on making Oobleck, which I did with second graders in Public School _____. The artifacts are the science lesson plan, which includes a mini math lesson on measurement, two language arts lesson plans, student work including an experience chart, and stories written by the children.

This lesson plan and the description and evaluation of the hands-on science activity show my knowledge of the science content and science process skills including observation, classification, measuring, and communication. The activity shows my ability to have children work in cooperative learning groups, and use inquiry skills to examine the Oobleck. It also shows my ability to develop an integrated unit with lessons in three curriculum areas (science, math, and language arts and literacy).

From this activity I learned that second grade children are able to work in cooperative learning groups very well if you give each member of the group something to do. I also learned that the children made very careful observations. They were able to measure independently using a recipe chart. They have very creative ideas and can create descriptive stories with interesting characters and plots.

These artifacts address NAEYC Standard 4. Using Developmentally Effective Approaches to Connect Children and Families such as hands-on science and inquiry; and Standard 5, Using Content Knowledge Building Meaningful Curriculum. They demonstrate my knowledge of science process skills, and tools of inquiry as I helped children test and observe the Oobleck, by asking, "What would happen if . . . ?" while they were testing the Oobleck. This was a very meaningful group of lessons for the children, teaching them about solids and liquids, their characteristics, and using a hands-on approach.

I have learned many lessons from this work that I will carry into the future. The integrated curriculum helps children learn because when you focus on a topic, each lesson builds on the skills and interest of the others and the skills have a context. When you use this approach, you include students with a wider variety of learning styles. Cooperative learning groups work when each member of the group has a responsibility.

You will notice that, in the rationale, the student used her answers to the questions in the artifact test. The rationale tells why the artifact represents the student, what she has learned, the standards addressed, and what she will take with her into the future. Next you will find the rationale written for a Showcase Portfolio.

- make careful observations and record their own data;

- describe and classify the ways in which the Oobleck were like liquids and like solids;

- measure independently;

- be imaginative, and able to create descriptive stories with interesting characters and plots.

These artifacts address NAEYC Standard 4 and Standard 5, and my knowledge of science content and science process skills, and tools of inquiry as I was helping children test and observe the Oobleck, by asking, "What would happen if . . . ?" I think this was a very meaningful group of lessons for the children. Their stories showed how much they learned about solids and liquids and how it stretched their imaginations.

The most important thing I learned was how the integrated curriculum helps children learn, with each lesson building on the others. The other important understanding was that cooperative learning groups work when each member of the group has a responsibility.

# Sample Rationale on Lesson Plans and Unit for E-Portfolio

Oobleck—An Integrated Curriculum conducted with second grade class in Public School_____, Brooklyn, New York

This group of artifacts include:

- a math lesson and reflection;
- a science lesson and reflection;
- a language and literacy lesson and reflection.

Evidence of student work including:

- charts;
- selected creative stories;
- cooperating teacher comments.

⇨ /□ ⇦

## What I Learned

From this activity I learned that:

- children work well in cooperative learning groups if given specific responsibilities;
- children are able to gather materials, observe, classify, experiment and collect data;
- children apply knowledge to a creative writing project.

**Upload digital photos of children's charted data, and selected stories here.**

⇨ |▢ ⇦

**Example of e-Portfolio Reflection on an Integrated Unit**

## The Standards Addressed

These artifacts address NAEYC Standard 4 Teaching and Learning and my knowledge of science content, science process skills, collected data, and tools of inquiry as I helped children experiment by asking "What if . . . ? questions" as they collected data, and applied that knowledge in a creative way.

**Upload the cooperating teacher's positive comments about the lesson here.**

**Example of e-Portfolio Reflection on an Integrated Unit**

**In my science and math lessons:**

- students measured ingredients;
- students observed and collected data on the characteristics of Oobleck;
- students dictated chart classifying characteristics they found in Oobleck

**Example of e-Portfolio Reflection on an Integrated Unit**

## What will I take into the future?

I will take into the future my understanding of the integrated curriculum and how each lesson built on the interest and ability of the one before, the abilities it taught, and the knowledge that children can work cooperatively if given responsibility and focus.

**Example of e-Portfolio Reflection on an Integrated Unit completed**

The e-portfolio tells the story of this student and her growth with her work supporting the rationale comments.

## Concluding Remarks

In this chapter you learned a reflective process that can serve you in any reflections you do throughout your life's work. You have also learned to use the reflective process to select the work that you will incorporate into your portfolio. This reflection will also help you to create the Rationale Statements that will accompany the artifacts in your portfolio, and become the glue that binds it together. Your rationale statements will now give nuance to your beliefs, and show the reader the thinking that went into your work. It will also tell the reader what you will take from this work into the future. Each rationale is your opportunity to tell, in your voice, part of the story of your becoming a teacher.

### What You Have Accomplished in This Chapter

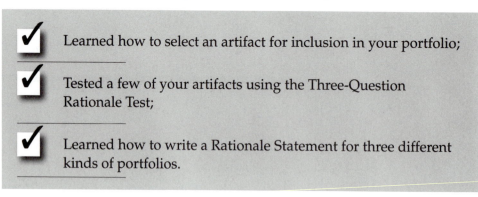

Learned how to select an artifact for inclusion in your portfolio;

Tested a few of your artifacts using the Three-Question Rationale Test;

Learned how to write a Rationale Statement for three different kinds of portfolios.

# Developing Your Portfolio

In this section you will develop your portfolio. If you are working on a developmental portfolio, you will be using Chapter 5. If you are creating a showcase portfolio, you will be using Chapter 6. If you are developing an e-portfolio, you will be using Chapter 7. For each kind of portfolio you are developing, these chapters will help you to:

- select artifacts appropriate to your portfolio;

- write rationales for the artifacts;

- prepare the artifacts for the portfolio;

- keep track of your progress;

- put all of the pieces together.

# The Developmental Portfolio

## Checklist of Things Needed

☐ Your Introductory Material (Table of Contents, Professional Goals Statement, Portfolio Statement of Purpose, Autobiography, Teaching Philosophy)

☐ The standards and/or competencies used by your teacher education program

☐ All of your artifacts (e.g., lesson plans, observations, workshop notes, research papers) organized into the sections of your Table of Contents

You will be constructing your portfolio and composing the story you will tell about your journey to becoming a teacher. The introductory pieces of the portfolio, which you have already created, will be tweaked and professionally prepared. The primary focus of this chapter will be to develop the main body of the portfolio. In earlier chapters, you have organized materials into categories and created a tentative Table of Contents. You have drafted your Professional Goals Statement, Portfolio Statement of Purpose, your Autobiography, your Teaching Philosophy, and have learned to select an artifact and write a Rationale Statement. Now, you will use those skills to put your entire portfolio together. In this chapter you will find a suggested list of materials that you may have and might include in your artifacts. However, the final selection of artifacts is yours to make. You must select pieces of work that represent you as a teacher. You must also be certain that you are following the guidance of your program, professors, director, or the licensing authority, which has devised the competencies and standards that you are demonstrating.

In the preceding chapter, the portfolio was described as telling a story about you and your development as a teacher. The metaphor of a story is important because as you compile this document you must be thinking about how each artifact is part of that story about you and your development. If you have any doubts about what your stated values, goals, and purpose are, go back and take a look at your Teaching Philosophy Statement, your Portfolio Purpose Statement, and your Professional Goals Statement. There you have laid out your reason(s) for creating the portfolio, and your thoughts about the teacher you are becoming. By reconnecting with your focus, you can look clearly at the work you have done, and say, "Does this piece represent me, my growth, and the teacher I am becoming and I hope to be?"

## Finding Your Story and Your Passion

Your Teaching Philosophy and your Professional Goals Statement should be uniquely you and reflect your passion for teaching. If you wrote those documents before you had a clear vision of your philosophical point of view as a teacher, you may wish to tweak them. Here are a few questions you can ask yourself to reflect on your developing point of view and focus the story you wish to tell as you assemble your portfolio. Most important, these are questions to help you express your passion so that your portfolio stands out from the rest.

### Reflection on the Picture of You

Look through your artifacts and think about the following questions:

1. What are you passionate about in teaching? A particular age group? A particular content area? An issue?

2. Do you have any particular interests, talents, or gifts, which you have discovered in your studies, that make you a better teacher (e.g., observing and recording, working with English language learners or special education students)?

3. What are the characteristics of the early childhood educators you have experienced (your own teachers, cooperating teachers) or learned about who have a philosophy that resonates for you? Why?

4. Of the teaching approaches you have read about, and discussed and tried, which ones do you expect to use in your teaching? Why?

5. Which methodologies have you found most satisfying and productive in your work with children? Why?

6. Of the educational issues you have discussed in class, is there one that you feel passionate about (e.g., parent involvement, multicultural education, special education issues such as mainstreaming, gender equity)? Why?

If your introductory material lacks passion and depth, by answering the preceding questions and tweaking your statements, you can focus it more on the picture of your development and who you are today. You want your introductory material to set the stage for the developing portrait of you as a teacher. Your Autobiography, your Professional Goals Statement, your Portfolio Goals Statement, and your Teaching Philosophy should not be about just any student, they should be about you specifically. Reread them. If they seem to be informative, but lack distinction, you may have to do a little tweaking. If you answer the above questions, you can add the interests, the discovered talents, and the passions, to these documents, which you have found as you have developed this work.

Once you find your passion, tweak your Philosophical Statement to include those characteristics that set you apart as a teacher. Use those ideas in your purpose statement and, if you see a place for them, your career goals and your Teaching Philosophy. If you have done very well in a particular area of study, toot your own horn. If, for example, you love psychology and have maintained a high G.P.A. in it, and you see the possibility of being a school psychologist or guidance counselor down the road, mention it in your Professional Goals Statement. If you have found a particular gift or talent, which makes you more valuable as a teacher, mention it in your Autobiography. If, for example, you have learned a foreign language that may be helpful in the schools in which you wish to teach, mention it. If you discovered a love for science in your science course and an internship and have a desire to teach science to children, mention it. The point is that the picture of you, which you create through your portfolio, should reflect the ideas and values that set you apart from the rest. With that picture in mind, we will build your portfolio by selecting your artifacts.

## Comprehensive List of Potential Artifacts

Here is a comprehensive list of the materials you might include in your portfolio. All of the work you do in connection with all of your courses are possible artifacts for inclusion in your portfolio.

(These are listed here alphabetically, but not in the order they should be placed in the portfolio.)

**Advocacy**   Evidence of work (voluntary or otherwise) for organizations which advocate for early childhood causes and programs, committee work for NAEYC, on behalf of Head Start, child care, the public library, science institutions, museums.

**Articles**   with reflective writing. Very often, in your education courses, you are given articles related to theory or issues and asked to read and write a reflective paper including analysis and your thoughts about the topic.

**Assessment tools**   and information, sample checklists, teacher-made inventories, teacher-made tests, or copies of children's work portfolios with your reflections on assessment and child development. These documents can demonstrate your knowledge of responsible assessment and knowledge of development of the whole child (physical, intellectual, emotional, and social).

**Books**   Teacher-made children's books (made by you), props, and materials used for teaching that you constructed. They should be well crafted.

**Certificates**   of completed training, workshops, seminars such as training in First Aid, Child Abuse and Neglect, Child Development Associate (CDA), Conflict Resolution.

**Child studies and observational logs,**   with the confidentiality of children protected (using pseudonyms or first initials).

**Classroom management**   strategies and materials you have created including sample charts (e.g., job charts, weather, cubby charts), and digital pictures of charts, choice boards, age-appropriate class schedules, and other organizing materials with your reflections on why they are good practice.

**Cooperative learning**   models and strategies that you have implemented and your reflections on this practice. Include your lesson or unit plans in which you utilized the strategy, with evidence of student work if possible (charts generated by students, lists, and collected data). Be sure to include in reflection why the strategy worked and how you might improve on it if you need to.

**Curriculum resources**   you have researched and developed, such as annotated bibliographies of children's books, sources of curriculum content posters, and sources of materials and/or equipment, Internet websites. These resources should have your annotations and reflections on how they would be used.

**Curriculum webs**   for integrated curriculum units or digital pictures of charts, digital pictures of student work, brainstorming notes on lessons and/or units, with the final lesson plan and evaluation.

**Curriculum workshop notes**   with reflections on what is learned and its application to practice.

**Discipline and/or guidance**   A philosophical statement on your views of guidance and discipline, and classroom community, with reflection papers on articles or books on the topic. For example, reflection papers on the issue of "Time Out" for which you have read articles pro and con. Resources such as lists of age and developmentally appropriate language that promotes positive self-image, activities, and materials that support emotional growth with your reflections on the topic.

**Displays,**   created by you, in connection with curriculum development projects and your teaching such as bulletin boards, poster boards, children's work, or cooperative learning group projects, can be preserved through pictures for your portfolio (digital photographs or video for your e-portfolio).

**Documentations**   of your accomplishments, including awards, certificates, honors, dean's list, scholarships, and transcripts.

**Essays,**   reflective papers on education topics that engage you in analysis on education and related issues.

**Evaluations**   of your teaching by professors, field supervisors, cooperating teachers.

**Internship**   logs and reflection papers.

**Issues in Education**   research and reflection papers (e.g., multicultural education, gender equity, race and class in education, mainstreaming, and special education)

**Journals**   of your own reflective writing for early childhood education courses. Children's journals, done under your teaching with your instructions, examples of children's work with your reflective writings.

**Lesson plans**   with description and reflective self-evaluation of the actual lesson, telling how you would improve on it and how you might follow it up. Include collected evidence of student work that accompanies the plans.

**Letters of Recommendation**   from professors, cooperating teachers, assistant principals, principals.

**Logs**   Reflective writing from field experiences and internships.

**Multicultural Education,**   **anti-bias resources** and materials and books that support including and embracing families from all cultures, races, religions, and sexual orientation with reflective writing and your philosophical statement.

**Parent and community involvement**   projects such as parent newsletters, parent interest surveys or inventories, workshop ideas, reflection papers on parent–teacher meetings, community resource lists, collected logs on parent workshops, and notes on parent workshops and/or school board meetings.

**Personal professional growth**  resources and artifacts such as memberships in professional organizations, and workshops or institutes you have attended given by professional organizations such as National Association for the Education of Young Children (NAEYC), National Science Teachers Association (NSTA), National Council of Teachers of Mathematics (NCTM), Child Care Inc, Zero to Three, National Council for the Social Studies.

**Photos**  of your work, including lessons, projects, and bulletin boards made from student work connected to lessons you planned and implemented.

**Portfolio Purpose Statement**  describing the kind of portfolio you are creating, and the intention or goal you have in creating the portfolio. (See Chapter 2.)

**Professional Goals Statement,**  which includes information on your short- and long-term career objectives. (See Chapter 3.)

**Research papers**  on topics related to early childhood education that reflect your ability to analyze and interpret information and apply it to practice. Action research you conduct on teaching projects. Research papers from related coursework in sociology, psychology, anthropology, or speech.

**Resume**  geared to the reader of the portfolio highlighting work experience with children, education, and scholarship including awards, certificates, or honors you have achieved.

**Room arrangement**  floor plans, pictures of floor plans models, or photographs of learning centers with reflective writing on age appropriateness. Lists of materials (age and grade appropriate) to extend and expand learning centers. Lists of special resources for materials and equipment.

**Special Education**  resources and ideas for mainstreaming and meeting needs of special students.

**Standards or Competencies**  A list of the standards and or competencies to which the work in the portfolio is being held.

**Student work**  Copies of student portfolios, or student work (with the child's confidentiality protected)—connected to lessons of units you conduct.

**Table of Contents**  It will list all of the sections and subsections of your portfolio. (See Chapter 2.)

**Teacher-made**  materials (well-crafted and suited to the skill being taught) games, songs, finger plays, and templates for game materials.

**Teaching philosophical statement(s)**  may include an overall teaching philosophy and/philosophical statements related to individual curricular areas such as science, social studies, or art. (See Chapter 3.)

**Technology resource lists** including annotations by you on developmentally appropriate and curriculum content-related websites for children and teacher resources for curriculum such as CDs and DVDs for areas such language and literacy, science, social studies, or math.

**Time Sheets** for each of your internships, field experiences, and student teaching. Reflective writing on lessons, curriculum workshops, visits to early childhood educational programs, or informal educational institutions.

**Videos** of your teaching, especially with your reflective writings on the lesson including what you would have improved upon.

## Select Your Artifacts

If you are assembling this developmental portfolio as you progress, it will be an opportunity to watch your abilities evolve and your resources grow. Each semester you will need to examine the work (essays, papers, projects) you have done in early childhood education courses, as well as your relevant psychology (child development, psychological disorders in young children), sociology, and anthropology (e.g., sociology of the family) and speech courses (speech disorders in children, storytelling and puppetry). Consider for inclusion in your portfolio: your internships, your research courses, your workshops and any reflective writing, and curriculum development projects done in connection with this work.

Earlier in the book an accordion file was recommended for keeping your work before you prepared it to be placed in the portfolio. You should also have plastic sleeves in which to secure your work to protect it, and so that you do not have to punch holes into the work to place it into the binder. All of the work that you place in your portfolio should be in good condition. Sometimes if you have stored a piece of work from a previous semester to put in to the portfolio, it is less than presentable. Occasionally accidents happen. If for some reason a piece of work important to your portfolio has been soiled, wrinkled, or stained, take the work to the professor whose grade is on the work, explain the problem, and ask permission to make a clean copy of the work, and ask for a signature or initials saying that this was permitted. This is especially true of time sheets because they are legal documents of time spent in a classroom. You do not want to be accused of photocopying work, which alters grades by a professor.

There are a few basic rules about the artifacts or pieces of work you should use:

1. The work should be typed and without major writing errors (e.g., grammar, punctuation, or spelling errors). This demonstrates that you are professional and have the skills and the abilities to teach.

2. The work should be yours, or in some way demonstrate your thinking.

3. The work should relate to your Purpose Statement and to your Teaching Philosophy.

There will be some artifacts that are not typed such as children's work, brainstorming charts or charts from curriculum projects, and handwritten journals. However, the rationale statements that accompany these artifacts should all be typed. Your work, such as research papers, reflective papers, lesson plans, and observational logs, should all be typewritten.

Very often students want to keep handouts of articles and other resource materials distributed by professors. If you see this piece as connected to your philosophy, and the understandings gained from it important to who you are as a teacher, you may keep it in your portfolio. However, you should include with it a reflective piece of writing that articulates what you have learned from it and why it is important to you as a teacher. If it is something you wish to keep for future reference, but not necessarily something that connects to your professionalism or your philosophy, file it in an accordion file called resources.

If you were following the suggestions in Chapter 2, you have sorted your artifacts into categories. You have also created a tentative Table of Contents, with the major sections or categories into which you have sorted your artifacts. Here is the suggested Table of Contents developed in Chapter 2:

---

**PORTFOLIO**

### Table of Contents

**Section 1. Introductory Information**

Personal Data (Name, Telephone, E-mail Address)

Portfolio Goal Statement

Professional Goals Statement

Resume

Autobiography

Teaching Philosophy

**Section 2. Child Development**

Observations

Child Studies

**Section 3. Curriculum and Teaching (Lesson Plans, Unit Plans, Curriculum Projects)**

Play

Dramatic Play

Blocks

Sand and Water

---

## Table of Contents (con't)

If you prefer the Table of Contents that the National Association for the Education of Young Children (NAEYC) Standards as a guide, you can find it here:

## PORTFOLIO

## Table of Contents

If you look at these tables of contents, they are like a Table of Contents in any of your textbooks. They are, in essence, outlines of topics into which you will place each artifact that you will include in your portfolio. Your task now is to take each artifact and decide whether it is a proper fit for your portfolio.

You can begin by labeling the inside cover of the portfolio binder, if you have not yet done so, with your name, telephone number, and e-mail address. If you lose it, someone can return it to you. Unfortunately, portfolios have been stolen and if you affix the label to the binder itself, you may prevent an unscrupulous person from taking it. You should also put a header and a footer on all of your work. If you have not been doing this all along, at least place it on your rationales as you create them.

The header should have your name and any identifying information you wish to give in order to recover your work should it be lost or stolen. If you type it in to the header section on your pull-down menu, it will appear on every page of your work. As it would require so much effort to remove it from each page of work, it should serve as a deterrent for anyone who would steal your work.

Here is an example of a header you might use that has your name, e-mail address, and college.

Jane Doe

E-mail address jane@ .com

E.C.E. Program, _____ College

Once the binder is labeled, you will place the items from the personal information section or introductory material into the binder. In this case, the first section is called Personal Information and will include:

Table of Contents

Portfolio Statement of Purpose

Professional Goals Statement

Resume

Autobiography

Teaching Philosophy

After you have tweaked the Portfolio Statement of Purpose, Professional Goals Statement, Resume, Autobiography, and Teaching Philosophy to reflect the picture of you, you can place those pieces in plastic sleeves and place them into your portfolio. Any certificates such as your Child Abuse and Neglect Certificate, First Aid, Violence Prevention, CDA, or any other certificate or honor that you have received should be placed into the portfolio. After the introductory material, you can begin to choose artifacts for the body of your portfolio. You can use the following Index sheet to keep track of the artifacts you include, and the standards you are addressing. You can begin by checking off the introductory material starting with the tentative Table of Contents. If there is no change of sections in the portfolio from now until its completion, the Table of Contents will remain the same. If you add a section, you can revise it. The sheet is intended to help you keep track of the work you have completed on your portfolio.

| Artifact | Entered Check | Rationale Draft/Completed | Standard or Competency |
|----------|---------------|---------------------------|------------------------|
|          |               |                           |                        |

The heading of each column is related to the artifacts that you will be including. The introductory material is listed for you in the following Index Sheet. You simply check off the introductory artifacts as you place them in the binder. There is no need for a rationale sheet for this introductory material, or for an entry into the standard or competency column. You will check off the Rationale Drafted/ Completed column, and the Standard or Competency column *only* for the artifacts of your work, such as your observations, lesson plans, and research papers.

## Artifact Index Sheet

| Artifact | Entered Check | Rationale Draft/Completed | Standard or Competency |
|---|---|---|---|
| Table of Contents | | | |
| Purpose Statement | | | |
| Personal Goals Statement | | | |
| Resume | | | |
| Autobiography | | | |
| Teaching Philosophy | | | |
| Teaching Video | | | |
| Honors | | | |
| | | | |
| | | | |
| **Transcript(s)** | | | |
| | | | |
| | | | |
| **Letters of Recommendation** | | | |
| | | | |
| | | | |
| **Child Development and Learning** | | | |
| | | | |
| **Building Family and Community Relationships** | | | |
| | | | |
| | | | |
| | | | |
| **Observing, Documenting, and Assessing to Support Young Children and Families** | | | |
| | | | |
| | | | |
| **Curriculum and Teaching (Lesson Plans, Unit Plans, Curriculum Projects)** <br>• **Using Developmentally Effective Approaches to Connect with Children and Families** <br>• **Using Content Knowledge to Build Meaningful Curriculum** | | | |
| | | | |
| | | | |
| | | | |
| | | | |
| | | | |
| | | | |

## Artifact Index Sheet (con't)

| Artifact | Entered Check | Rationale Draft/Completed | Standard or Competency |
|---|---|---|---|
| **Related Specialized Coursework Projects (Psych, Spec. Ed., Speech and Language)** | | | |
| | | | |
| | | | |
| | | | |
| **Research Papers** | | | |
| | | | |
| | | | |
| | | | |
| | | | |
| **Exams** | | | |
| | | | |
| | | | |
| | | | |
| **Professional Development (workshops, certificates, memberships in professional organizations)** | | | |
| | | | |
| | | | |
| **Miscellaneous** | | | |
| | | | |
| | | | |
| | | | |

Next you will assemble the artifacts that are the body of your work.

## Applying the Rationale Test to Your Artifacts

You need to decide which of all of these artifacts represents your progression from beginning student to who you are as a novice teacher, and what you value as a professional. As you look at the work you might see pieces that represent leaps of progress in your knowledge and abilities as a teacher. For example, there may be logs you had written that represent finally understanding objective recording. You may have had the experience of writing your first, well-organized lesson plan. Place the work in each category in the order of your development. With each piece that you think is potentially one for your portfolio, give it the Rationale Test that you used to learn about choosing an artifact and writing a rationale statement in Chapter 4, by answering these three questions:

1. What is this artifact and what did you do to develop it? (What?)

2. How does this artifact demonstrate my growth as a professional and help me meet the standards? (So What?)

3. How will I use what I have learned in the future? (Now What?)

Answer the three questions in writing, do not assume you know the answers. This process will tell you first whether it is a good selection, and whether it meets the standards that you are trying to reach. It will also tell you whether, from the work, you have learned something that is meaningful to you as a teacher. If, as you are holding the artifact up to that standard, you should find that it represents you well, check "in" on the top of the sheet, and use your notes on the Rationale Test sheet to write the rationale. If you find that a particular artifact is not appropriate because it does not say anything important about you as a teacher, does not meet your competencies and demonstrate your growth as a professional, check the space that says "out." Write a brief reason for its rejection. The reason you do this is so that you keep track of each artifact and your thinking on whether it should be included. The last thing you want to do, is look at a piece of work and say to yourself, "Did I want to include this?" I think I said no, but I don't recall why. If you make this brief written note, you do not have to look critically at the piece again and waste valuable time.

Once you are finished rating the piece and deciding whether it is good for your portfolio, you have almost finished the work on your rationale. The notes that are the answers to the three questions will be the basis for your rationale statement.

## RATIONALE TEST

Artifact _____ Date _____ In _____ Out _____

Reason for Rejection _____

| 1 |
| --- |
| 1. What is this artifact and what did you do to develop it? (What?) |
| 2 |
| 2. How does this artifact demonstrate my growth as a professional and how does it help me meet the standards? (So What?) |
| 3 |
| 3. How will I use what I have learned in the future? (Now What?) |

If you have a group of similar pieces of work that relate to the same standards, (e.g., observational logs related to assessment) group them together, one right after the other, because you will find that the work goes much quicker. You will remember the standards and what is of value to you based on that standard. You will also gain practice in articulating how the artifact helps you to meet the standard, and what you have learned from the work. If you have a few pieces of work that go together, such as logs on the same child (child study), or lessons in a unit, you might be able to write just one rationale for the grouping.

## Connection of Standards and Competencies to Your Artifacts

If you have any difficulty understanding the standard or the competency that you believe your work is related to and how your work connects to the standard, write out your understanding of the standard or competency. You can deconstruct (take apart) the standard by asking yourself the following questions:

- What knowledge does this artifact focus on?

- What skills or abilities did I gain in this work that relates to this standard or competency?

If you think about these questions, you should be able to better understand the standard or competency and how your work is connected to it.

For example:

> A student took a trip to a science museum, and wrote a reflection paper on both the trip, and how she would use the trip in her own teaching. She wrote a lesson plan in science connected to the exhibit she viewed. She took a child with her on a second trip to conduct the lesson with the child. She reflected on the experience.

The student knows that the work has something to do with NAEYC Learning Standard 5, Using Content Knowledge to Build Meaningful Curriculum. She reads Standard 5. It seems to be the standard she relates this work to but she thinks it may also be connected to Standard 4.

### Standard 4. Using Developmentally Effective Approaches to Connect with Children and Families

Students prepared in early childhood degree programs understand that teaching and learning with young children is a complex enterprise, and its details vary depending on children's ages, characteristics, and the settings within which teaching and learning occur. They understand and use positive relationships and supportive interactions as the foundation for their work with young children and families. Students know, understand, and use a wide array of developmentally appropriate approaches, instructional strategies, and tools to connect with children and families and positively Influence each child's development and learning.

### Key elements of Standard 4

**4a:** Understanding positive relationships and supportive interactions as the foundation of their work with children

**4b:** Knowing and understanding effective strategies and tools for early education

**4c:** Using a broad repertoire of developmentally appropriate teaching/learning approaches

**4d:** Reflecting on their own practice to promote positive outcomes for each child

She looks at the competencies in her science course, and it says,

> The student will learn to write lesson plans using an integrated approach. The student will learn about teaching strategies such as the inquiry approach, science journals, hands on learning, and cooperative learning. The student will learn an inquiry-based approach to learning science content and the science process. The student will understand the science process skills and how to have children explore them.

## Deconstructing a Standard or Competency

The student answers the following two questions:

| What knowledge does this artifact focus on? |
| --- |
| Writing lesson plans, because I wrote a lesson plan that was an integrated unit with a language arts and social studies lesson to include the trip. 4. |
| Learning science content, because I learned about whales (kinds, sizes, bearing live young). 5 |
| Understanding science process skills, observation, classification, and communication, included in my lesson plan. 5 |
| Understanding the inquiry approach. 5, |
| The research of resources and books for curriculum. 5 |

| What did I do (what skills and abilities did I use) in this work that helped me to learn this competency or move closer to the standard? |
| --- |
| I observed and learned about the whale exhibit and the science content. I developed the lesson plan with a good "big idea" about the needs of living things, and leading questions. 5 |
| I created the activity worksheets that helped children draw their observations and take notes, and ask their own questions (inquiry). 5 |
| I evaluated the lesson plan and said how I would improve upon it. 4 |
| I reflected on, and assessed, the children's work. 5 |
| I reflected on my own work. 4 |
| NAEYC Standards 4b, c, d, 5a, b, c |

As you think about a standard or a competency, you can deconstruct it by thinking about the skills the standard or competency requires. As you answer the two questions, you should be identifying the individual skills, abilities, and pieces of knowledge that you engaged in as you did the work evidenced in this artifact. The work should either move you closer to the standards or the competencies set by your early childhood program and by your professors. For the previous notes the student used the competencies on her syllabus to think about her work and the skills involved in it.

If your college is not using the NAEYC Standards, look on your syllabus. The syllabus usually has a list of competencies, skills, and abilities that you will gain as a result of taking the course.

If you are still unsure whether you understand the competency and the connection to the standard, it is quite likely that you need to talk with someone. You may wish to discuss the competency with a peer or your professor. Ask a professor or a peer to review whether your understanding of your work meshes with the competency or standard you relate it to. Discuss the elements of the competency to be sure you understand it. For example, a syllabus may state that you will learn to write a lesson plan. The syllabus might list elements of a good lesson plan such as the motivation, objectives, leading questions, and follow-up activity. The elements of a good observation are objective language and detailed description. Each artifact represents work that has particular competencies and standards of performance set by your professors, directors, and the professional and licensing authority. Remember, as you begin to study the language of any profession, there is jargon (use of vocabulary particular to that profession), which you might have difficulty understanding. Do not let this be a cause for worry. Every profession—medicine, law, computer science, education—has its own jargon.

Over time, you will become familiar with the jargon most often used by early childhood educators. By talking about the competencies and their relationship to the standards, you should gain a better understanding of their meaning, and the reasons for them.

## Write Your Rationales

For every artifact you wish to place in the portfolio, perform the three-question test. If the artifact passes the test, then use the answers to the questions to write a rationale statement. There are examples of rationale statements in Chapter 3. Those sample rationale statements are related to artifacts that are either observations or lesson plans and unit plans. Here is another example of work that students might do in the first years of study. It is a rationale test and sample rationale for a paper about a visit to a Montessori School.

> This first-year student did an oral report on Maria Montessori, and visited a Montessori school to learn, firsthand, about this early childhood model. She wrote a reflection paper on the visit, and drew a floor plan of the classroom. She described the activity that she saw, and documented the visit with a paper on the number of children, the adult–child ratio, an observation of the activity, and reflection on what she had learned.
> The artifact she wants to test is the paper.

Following are the notes she made on her Rationale Test, and the sample Rationale Statement she wrote based on the notes. The sample Rationale Statement follows.

---

**RATIONALE TEST**

Artifact Reflection on Montessori School Visit Date _____

In _____ X _____ Out _____

Reason for Rejection _____

**1. What is this artifact and what did you do to develop it? (What?)**

This artifact is a reflective paper on an early childhood model program. I have researched early childhood models firsthand. I am able to reflect and compare this classroom to others I have seen and worked in. I am becoming more knowledgeable about early childhood models and the different roles of the teacher, schedules, and activities for children.

---

**2. How does this artifact demonstrate my growth as a professional and how does it help me meet the standards? (So What?)**

I have learned, through research and firsthand experience, about the Montessori approach.

This artifact is one of my first attempts at reflective writing. I was able to compare this model to the childcare center I visited, looking at room arrangement, and the teacher's role.

NAEYC 1. I think I have learned about an early childhood model that is respectful of children and their needs.

**4.** This standard says that I should be able to use approaches that are developmentally appropriate. This visit helps me to have an approach, which lets each individual child choose his or her activities, and work at his or her own pace, and prepares the room with a number of materials for all of the different needs.

**3. How will I use what I have learned in the future? (Now What?)**

I have learned, through research and firsthand experience, about the Montessori approach.

This artifact is one of my first attempts at reflective writing, which I will use in the future. When I compare this model to the childcare centers I visited, I learned to make room arrangement support the child's independence; and to observe children as they work and in order to plan.

---

**RATIONALE STATEMENT FOR REFLECTION
ON MONTESSORI SCHOOL VISIT**

This research paper on Montessori shows my study of early childhood models, and that I have studied the Montessori classroom firsthand. I am very interested in the similarities and differences in the different models. In this reflection I compare this classroom to others that I have seen and in which I worked. I am becoming more knowledgeable about different early childhood approaches. This artifact is one of my first attempts at reflective writing and I received positive feedback from my professor on the details I noticed.

This work helps me to meet NAEYC Standard 1, in that I have learned about an early childhood model and approach that is respectful of children and their needs. I have also moved closer to meeting Standard 4, because this standard says that I should be able to use approaches that are developmentally appropriate, and the Montessori approach helps me to assist each individual child to choose his activities, and to move at his own pace. It also shows how to prepare materials for all of their different needs.

I will use the positive ideas I found in the Montessori classrooms in the classrooms in which I teach in the future. I plan to let children choose the materials they want to play with at choice time, to have an organized and prepared environment in which they can play, to treat each child as an individual, and to observe and learn from them.

You will notice that the words in the Rationale Test are the notes for the rationale statement. If you type this on the computer, you can copy and paste the answers and simply edit to be sure that you do not repeat material.

Here is one more example of a student's work, with the rationale test, and sample Rationale Statement.

This third-year student had to create a community resource list for a course in school and community. She developed an extensive list and visited many of the resources to give updated information on the services, personnel, and contact information. She also wrote a reflection paper to describe what she learned and to tell how the assignment affected her.

You will see her notes on the Rationale Test and her sample rationale statement that follows.

**RATIONALE TEST**

Artifact __ Community Resource List ____ Date _____ In _____ Out _____

Reason for Rejection _____

**1. What is this artifact and what did you do to develop it? (What?)**

This is an annotated resource list that I compiled with services for children and families in the neighborhood surrounding my internship placement. It demonstrates that I am able to research a community to support children and their families. I can reach out to community organizations and get to know the people who are there for children and families. I am a teacher who cares about the children and families whom I serve.

**2. How does this artifact demonstrate my growth as a professional and how does it help me meet the standards? (So What?)**

This artifact demonstrates my ability to recognize the importance of families and communities in the lives of children. It demonstrates my ability to work with other professionals in the community as part of a team.

**3. How will I use what I have learned in the future? (Now What?)**

I have given my resource list to the neighborhood school, and to the pre-kindergarten at which I interned. I expect to use the skills that I have learned to research the neighborhoods in which I teach, and to reach out to the community organizations who serve the children I teach and their families. I will ask them to send me flyers and updates on activities, and will post them in parent rooms and pass them on to the parent's association.

## COMMUNITY RESOURCE LIST RATIONALE STATEMENT

I researched and compiled this community resource list in connection with the course School and Community 301. As I researched the many programs listed here, I was excited about the information that I was collecting and how it might help the families with whom I worked. The work shows my ability to study a community and find out about the resources available to support the children I teach and their families. I was able to reach out to community organizations (e.g., the neighborhood library, museums, legal aid, food banks, voter registration), and get to know the key people who provide services to children and families.

This artifact demonstrates my ability to recognize the importance of families and communities in the lives of children. It also helps me to meet Standard 2 Building Family and Community Relationships as I learned to work with other professionals in the community as part of a team.

I am very proud of the fact that my resource list is a resource for parents in the Universal Pre-kindergarten program at which I interned. I expect to use the skills I have learned to research the neighborhoods in which I teach, and to reach out to the community organizations that serve the families of the children I teach. I will ask them to send me flyers and updates on activities, and I will post them in parent rooms and pass them on to the parent associations.

Now it is your turn. If you think about it, there are four easy steps to assembling your work.

1. Select the artifact and conduct the Rationale Test.

2. Use the answers to test an artifact for inclusion.

3. Copy and paste notes on the rationale sheet to write the first draft of your rationale.

4. Edit the Rationale Statement.

Now, simply do this for the artifacts that you have and for those that you are ready to place into the portfolio.

One by one, you can look at the pieces of work and ask whether it helps show my development, and represents my goals, and my abilities as a teacher. Then, for any piece that you think fits that picture, use the Rationale Test. By applying that test, you will arrive at those things you have learned, the standards you have tried to meet, and what you will take with you into the future.

## Prepare for Presentation

All of your work should be professionally presented. You should have Rationale Statements for each artifact or group of artifacts that you want to include in the portfolio. Be sure you have proofread, spell checked, and grammar checked your Rationale Statements. Give the Rationale Statements a title (e.g. Rationale Statement for Reflection on **Visit to Montessori School**), date, and whatever formatting your program requires. If there is none, you can use this generic format.

June __, 20__

Rationale Statement for

"Reflection on a Visit to Montessori School"

By Jane Doe

NAEYC Standards Addressed: 1 and 4b

*[The Rationale statement goes here.]*

With the advent of computers and the availability of a variety of fonts, patterns for creating block print, arched designs, clip art, and many other graphic design features, students sometimes want to decorate their document's cover pages with some graphic design. You should focus first on the content of your work rather than how many bells and whistles you can put on the cover. Keep it simple and consistent. If you put a simple line border on your rationale page, use it for all of the rationale sheets so that there is a consistency in the document. If you select an icon or graphic image to signify a particular category of artifact, or a particular kind of document, try to have it complement the work, not detract from it. The graphic should not be the focus of attention. Your work, your development, and your ideas about teaching and learning should be the focus. Principals, directors, and professors are interested in your ideas about child development, and teaching, not how many clip art pictures you can access. So keep it simple.

Place the Rationale Sheet in a plastic sleeve, and place the artifact in its own plastic sleeve(s). Place them into your binder in the appropriate section. Although it may have taken awhile to learn this process, once you understand it, your work should go very quickly. However, do not take short cuts on the care you put into your work and your attention to detail just to do it quickly. Take care to do it well.

Once you place the document in the portfolio, write its name on the Artifact Index Sheet. List the name of the artifact, the date you entered it, check off if the Rationale is a draft, or completed, and the Standard or Competency to which the artifact relates. The purpose of these notations is that sometimes you are working on the portfolio and need to stop. If you quickly note where you are with an artifact, you won't have to redo the work and the analysis to get up to speed when you begin again.

## Artifact Index Sheet

| Artifact | Entered Check | Rationale Draft/Completed | Standard or Competency |
|---|---|---|---|
| Table of Contents | | | |
| Purpose Statement | | | |
| Personal Goals Statement | | | |
| Resume | | | |
| Autobiography | | | |
| Teaching Philosophy | | | |
| Teaching Video | | | |
| Certificates and Honors | | | |
| | | | |
| | | | |
| **Transcript(s)** | | | |
| | | | |
| | | | |
| **Letters of Recommendation** | | | |
| | | | |
| | | | |
| **Child Development** | | | |
| | | | |
| | | | |
| | | | |

# Artifact Index Sheet (con't)

| Artifact | Entered Check | Rationale Draft/Completed | Standard or Competency |
|---|---|---|---|
| **Curriculum and Teaching (Lesson Plans, Unit Plans, Curriculum Projects)** | | | |
| | | | |
| | | | |
| | | | |
| | | | |
| | | | |
| **Related Specialized Coursework Projects (Psychology, Special Education, Speech and Language)** | | | |
| | | | |
| | | | |
| | | | |
| **Research Papers** | | | |
| | | | |
| | | | |
| | | | |
| | | | |
| **Exams** | | | |
| | | | |
| | | | |
| | | | |
| **Professional Development (workshops, certificates, memberships in professional organizations)** | | | |
| | | | |
| | | | |
| **Miscellaneous** | | | |
| | | | |
| | | | |
| | | | |

If, as you complete your coursework, and you work on the rationale statements, you will find that it will not take a great deal of time to complete them. All of the skills and abilities you are learning in these courses will be fresh in your mind, so it will be easier for you to articulate the rationale. Unfortunately, most students wait until a portfolio review in the second or third year of college to complete this work and then they have to pull an all-nighter writing rationales for three semesters of work. This is much more difficult, because you have to remember what the skills and competencies were that you were learning during your earlier work. You have to recreate the reflective ideas and emotions that say what the work meant to you. This is almost impossible. This kind of catch-up work is not authentic. It does not support your work to become a professional. Work on your portfolio each semester. Construct it as you construct yourself as a teacher. Do the reflection about your work while it is fresh in your mind. Capture the pride in your accomplishments, and the joy in your success in your development as a professional.

### Prepare a Cover Page

You will want to develop a cover page. You may ask why you didn't prepare a cover page at the beginning of the process, instead of now when you are at its end. The answer is that when you began, your picture of yourself and your portfolio was incomplete. You were still constructing it. Now you know who you are as a teacher, and you have the portrait you wanted to build. At this point, all you need to do is find the proper frame for it. You must now design a cover page, and give it a title that represents you. You can use Microsoft Word or PowerPoint. If you use Word, you will notice that under "Insert menu," you can insert clip art, photos, Word Art (text in different designs). You can design a cover page using PowerPoint using a slide that blocks print, and allows you to insert photos and clip art that represents you.

**PowerPoint cover page example.**

You built your developmental portfolio, piece by piece, as you completed the work in Chapter 5. You also refined and edited your Autobiography and Teaching Philosophy. As you did this reflection you reconnected with the theories and practices that made you into the teacher you have become. You finalized and placed your Table of Contents into your portfolio, and selected the work you wanted for each section. You analyzed your work, looking at the competencies you developed and how they met the standards of the profession. You crafted the Rationale Statements to accompany each piece of work, based on your reflections and analysis, which helped clarify your thinking and revealed that thinking for the reader. Finally, you have created a cover page for your work, which will present your portfolio to the public.

Your developmental portfolio represents a great deal of work completed over two or four years. It is a major accomplishment in your journey toward becoming a teacher. As the work in this document may still grow and change, as you mature as a teacher, this is a time to take stock and appreciate your achievement of your goal.

## What You Have Accomplished in This Chapter

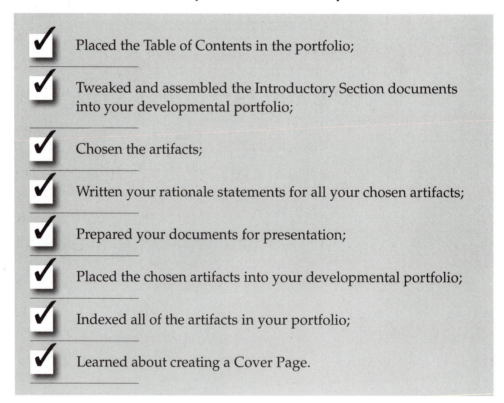

✔ Placed the Table of Contents in the portfolio;

✔ Tweaked and assembled the Introductory Section documents into your developmental portfolio;

✔ Chosen the artifacts;

✔ Written your rationale statements for all your chosen artifacts;

✔ Prepared your documents for presentation;

✔ Placed the chosen artifacts into your developmental portfolio;

✔ Indexed all of the artifacts in your portfolio;

✔ Learned about creating a Cover Page.

# The Showcase Portfolio

## Checklist of Things Needed for Chapter 6

☐ Your Introductory Material (Table of Contents, Autobiography, Professional Goals Statement, Resume, Portfolio Statement of Purpose, Teaching Philosophy)

☐ The standards and/or competencies used by your teacher education program

☐ Your Developmental Portfolio if you are drawing work from that to create the Showcase

☐ All your artifacts (e.g., lesson plans, observations, workshop notes, research papers) organized into the sections of your Table of Contents

In this chapter you will create a showcase portfolio. You will select pieces of work and connect them so that they construct a portrait of who you are as a teacher at this juncture of your career. Unlike the developmental portfolio, which is the story of your development and journey to becoming a teacher, this portfolio is the portrait of who you are today. A portrait has detail and nuance. A portrait takes time to compose, and time to develop. It represents the fullness and the richness of the subject. Your job, as you compose this portfolio, is to develop a rich, nuanced picture of yourself as a teacher. In this portrait, you will want to be sure that a comprehensive view of your teaching abilities is highlighted. Unlike an artist who creates with paint or pastels, you compose with words. Your portrait will be told as a story that depicts the many qualities, dispositions, abilities, values, and beliefs that you bring to teaching.

As you select work that will represent you, you must be aware of the reader of this portfolio, because the reader(s) does not have a great deal of time to study the showcase portfolio. The reader(s) might be an employer such as a principal, a director, or even a professor in your education program or the graduate program to which you are applying. The reader may be an official of a licensing or certifying body. It is important, therefore, that you choose artifacts that represent you well. You want to be sure that your work is presented with rationales, for each piece, that reveal aspects of you and your abilities as a teacher.

If you did the work in the earlier chapters, you have already created the introductory pieces of personal information for the portfolio. You have drafted your Professional Goals Statement, your Portfolio Purpose Statement, your Autobiography, and your Teaching Philosophy. You have learned to choose an artifact and to write a Rationale Statement. Now you will tweak, and professionally prepare, that Introductory Material, and place it in the portfolio. You will also develop the body of the portfolio by selecting artifacts and writing rationales that portray your talents and abilities as a teacher.

The artifacts you choose, which represent your abilities, create the portrait of you as a teacher. However, what holds the work together are the rationales, or your reflective writings, that tell the reader who you are, what you believe, and what you value. Your ideas and beliefs about teaching and learning, are what set you apart from others. They are the things that will have a professor, principal, or a director remember you. Therefore, your portrait must not only highlight good work, but that work must be connected to who you are, and the ideas you hold about teaching.

Your initial ideas about who you are will be in the introductory material in your Teaching Philosophy, your Professional Goals Statement, and the Portfolio Purpose Statement. If you have any doubts about what your stated values, goals, and purposes are, go back and take a look at these Introductory Materials. There you have laid out your reason for creating the portfolio, as well as your thoughts about the teacher you have become. If you feel that your philosophy has evolved since you wrote those documents, you can tweak your statements. In the next few pages, you will have the opportunity to take a second reflective look at yourself and your passion. See whether there are aspects of yourself to be added to those initial views of you as a teacher. By reconnecting with your focus, you can look clearly at the work you have done and ask, "Does this piece represent me, and the teacher that I am becoming and that I hope to be? Is this portfolio presenting a multifaceted picture of what I say about who I am, what I believe, and what I value as a professional?"

## Choosing Your Best Artifacts

In the showcase portfolio, you are exhibiting work, at a point in your development that says you have acquired a certain amount of knowledge, skills, and abilities, as proof that you are a teacher. Typically, you will be preparing this portfolio at the end of either your associate or bachelor's degree. It is a showcase, or capstone, portfolio, because you are at a phase wherein you have a body of work, and experience with different aspects of teaching. You have learned about developing curriculum, planning lessons, and evaluating the lessons you have implemented. You have learned something about child development, and the theories and philosophies that are the underpinnings of the profession. You have learned about responsible assessment, observation, and recording children's behaviors objectively. You will be submitting evidence of this work to demonstrate your competency for graduation, for employment, and for certification or licensing. You, therefore, should be selective and provide only the best of your work.

But what does the best mean? The best can mean a great many things. What is "best" can be determined by answering the following questions:

- Does this work meet performance standards and required competencies of my teacher education program?
- Does this work meet national professional standards?
- Does this work have a positive effect on children?
- Does this work demonstrate initiative?
- Is this work innovative?
- Does this work demonstrate commitment to the profession?

The best work may mean the best work that meets the standards set by your professors and your college's early childhood program. This will be determined by your grades, professors' comments and evaluations, field and student teacher evaluations, and performance standards on rubrics. If you are in a teacher education program that conforms to the guidelines of the national professional associations, such as the National Association for the Education of Young Children (NAEYC), and the National Council for Accreditation of Teacher Education (NCATE), and/or the Interstate New Teacher Assessment and Support Consortium (INTASC), the standards set in your teacher education courses will conform to the national standards established by these bodies. However, as a professional, or as someone entering the profession, you should become aware of the standards, and through the self-assessment process of developing this portfolio, engage yourself in judging your work against the standards that the profession holds dear. Your best work then, will be the work assessed by you as meeting the standards.

Your best work may be judged by the effect it has had on children. For example, if a lesson or unit resulted in exemplary work by children (e.g., art work, data collection, writing, and journals), that can be a measure of best work. This is evidenced in your work, which will consist of the curriculum project, the lesson plans, the methods and the strategies you employed while teaching, the evidence of the children's work, and the comments of your field supervisors and cooperating teachers. Your reflections on the work and/or your evaluations and ideas for improvement would also be good evidence of whether this work has taught you about, not only the performance of these children, but of the performances of the children who you will teach in the future.

If your work demonstrates initiative that goes above and beyond the usual parameters that students typically take on, this may be considered best work. For example, a small group of students assigned to do a field experience in a public school saw the need for activities for children after breakfast. They asked permission to bring in books to create story time and reading circles for the early childhood grades. This activity contributed to the school community. If documented through reflective writing and letters by a professor and school administrators, this activity, because of the initiative that the students showed in coming up with the idea and implementing it in a consistent way, can be considered best work.

Your work may be innovative, in that you came up with a new and more effective way of doing something. For example, a student interning in an infant and toddler program had the idea of taking pictures of baby's activities (eating peas, taking first steps, drawing with crayons, turning pages of a book) and sending them home with babies. The director loved the idea because it added to the home-school connection and building relationships with the family. This can be documented in reflective writing about how the project evolved. You could also document the reactions of parents to the project, and document the evaluations of your cooperating teacher, and director and field supervisor as well.

Another barometer for judging work to be best is that it demonstrates commitment to the profession of teaching, and to early childhood education. For example, if a student becomes interested in supporting legislation to improve funding for child care, Head Start, or public education, she might begin a letter-writing campaign to legislators. She might also write a research paper or reflective paper on the issue. Included in such a paper would be a discussion about the process of developing the letter and identifying constituencies for support. Having done these things could make the student's work in this area a strong candidate for best work. As you can see there are many ways of determining what demonstrates your best work. As you look at your work, you need to say, "What demonstrates what is best about me?

What artifacts showcase my best qualities as a teacher? What artifacts create the best portrait of me? Which set me apart from others?"

In order to focus on the qualities that set you apart, do the following reflection. It will help you to take a fresh look at your introductory pieces of work such as your Goals Statement, Teaching Philosophy, and Portfolio Purpose Statement.

### Reflection on the Picture of You

1. What are you passionate about as a teacher (a particular age group, a particular curriculum content, an issue)? Why?

2. Which philosophies and theories have you adopted in your work as part of your Teaching Philosophy? Why?

3. Of the teaching approaches you have read about, and discussed, which ones do you expect to use in your teaching, and why?

4. How are your Teaching Philosophy and favored approaches evidenced in your work?

5. Which methodologies have you found most satisfying and productive in your work with children? Why?

6. What educational issues (parent involvement, multicultural education, special education or issues such as mainstreaming, equity in science and math education, and technology) do you feel passionate about? How does your work reflect that passion?

7. Do you have any particular interests, talents, or gifts that are revealed in your work as a teacher (observing and recording, working with English Language Learners, special education, science education, math education)?

8. What are your best qualities as a teacher?

Remember, your Teaching Philosophy, your Professional Goals Statements, and the Portfolio Purpose Statement will set the stage for the pieces of work that will showcase you as a teacher. Therefore, before you select the work, you should find your passion and your particular interests to include in your introductory material. You want it to include those characteristics that set you apart as a teacher, and that create, for a prospective employer, graduate school, or your professors, your story. Use the ideas from the "Reflection on the Picture of You" list to enhance your Purpose Statement and your Goals Statement. If you have done very well in a particular area of study, talk about your successes. If, for example, you have an interest in teaching English as a Second Language learners, focus on that. If you have already been accepted to a masters program, mention it. If you have found particular gifts or talents, that make you more valuable as a teacher, mention them in your Autobiography. If, for example, you have learned a foreign language that may be helpful in the schools in which you wish to teach, mention it. If you discovered a love for math or science, social studies, or literacy, in your curriculum coursework or internships and have developed games or other learning materials, state it in your Teaching Philosophy. The point is that the portrait of you, which you create through your portfolio, should reflect the ideas and values that make you a distinctive, unique teaching professional. With that picture in mind, you will build your portfolio by selecting your artifacts.

## Let Your Artifacts Show a Range of Ability

In the showcase portfolio you will choose artifacts that demonstrate a range of your abilities as a teacher. Rather than showing many individual lesson plans, or observation logs, your focus here should be broader and more comprehensive. You should consider, for example, showing a child study, which demonstrates a body of work to assess a child's development and to understand responsible assessment in early childhood. You might also consider presenting a curriculum unit plan with a few lesson plans, a video of you teaching one of them, and a reflective evaluation of the children's work, and of your teaching. This shows your ability to construct curriculum, plan lessons, and implement and assess the success of your teaching performance. If you showcase your research, choose a work which demonstrates your scholarship and knowledge of resources, but that also shows aspects of your philosophy and point of view. The idea is to create a rich, multifaceted, view of you for the reader.

As you select artifacts, be especially aware of the requirements you must meet. You must be certain that you are following the guidance of your program, professors, director, or the licensing authority, which have devised the competencies and standards you are demonstrating. In showcase portfolios, there may be required pieces of work that you must submit. Leaving out any required piece can result in failure to meet the requirements. Even if the rest of your work is exemplary, if it is incomplete because a required piece is missing, it can mean failure.

In the chapter on the developmental portfolio there is an extensive list of artifacts that are possible choices for you as you develop the showcase portfolio. Look through that list to see the variety of possibilities for your portfolio. Here is a short list, drawn from the earlier list, of the artifacts that might showcase your work as a teacher. The following pieces can give a comprehensive view of a variety of aspects of your teaching abilities:

**Child Study,** with selected observational logs of a child over time, interview protocol with notes, and summary log or report, evidence of the child's work, reflection on what you have learned about child development and responsible assessment.

**Curriculum Unit Plan,** with curriculum web, brainstorming, selected lesson plans, video of your teaching the lesson, evaluation of the lesson, selected pieces of children's work.

**Curriculum Resource Annotated Lists,** which collect teaching and learning resources that you will use in your teaching. The annotation should be done by you and relate to the curriculum area and the conceptual material you are illustrating. Examples of these annotated lists might be: a list of science websites with curriculum ideas and content in early childhood primary grades, and an annotated bibliography with author studies of children's books and potential lesson ideas.

**Community and Parent Involvement Projects,** including newsletters, parent informational handbooks, letters, flyers, parent workshop designs, parent interest surveys or inventories, annotated lists of parent education materials (brochures, tracts, booklets, posters) and annotated lists of community resources.

**Research Papers** on early childhood education issues, theoretical approaches, or projects in fields such as psychology, anthropology, and sociology that relate to education. Teacher action research conducted while implementing a teaching project with children with children's work examples, and your analysis of your teaching.

## Important Note on Confidentiality and Protecting the Identity of Children

In Chapter 5, on Developmental Portfolios we stated that you must protect the identity of children if you store their work, or observations or child studies of them in your portfolio. In early childhood education, the confidentiality of children's records including their names and other identifiable characteristics is of utmost concern. Any artifacts that you use in your portfolio that are related to children, **must not** include information that reveals their identity. Therefore, use pseudonyms or initials on observations or child studies of children or on children's work and not their real names. Photographs should be done shooting over the shoulder of the child without showing their faces. Classes and room numbers should be removed from digital photos of bulletin boards. If you do use a photo of a child's face, you must get the parent's permission before publishing it in your portfolio. Later we will discuss e-portfolios which can be available on the Internet. There, especially, it is of utmost importance to protect children's identities.

## Select Your Artifacts

It was suggested earlier, that you collect and store your work in a binder organized into categories. If you have not already done so, you should protect your work in plastic sleeves. Be sure that all the work is in pristine condition. If a any of your artifacts has been soiled, wrinkled, or stained, take the work to the professor whose grade is on it, and ask permission to make a clean photocopy of the work. Be sure to get the signature or initials of your instructor granting permission to include the photocopied version. This is especially true of time sheets, which are legal documents showing time spent in a classroom or learning institution, and which require signatures giving permission if they are replicated.

There are a few rules about the artifacts that you should adhere to, especially in a showcase portfolio:

1. The work should be typed and without major writing errors (e.g., grammar, punctuation, spelling). This says that you are professional and have the skills and the abilities to teach.

2. The work should be yours, or in some way demonstrate your thinking.

3. The work should relate to your Purpose Statement and to your Teaching Philosophy.

You may have some artifacts that are not typed such as children's work, brainstorming, charts from curriculum projects, or handwritten journals. However, the Rationale Statements, which accompany these artifacts, should all be typed. Your work such as research papers, reflective papers, lesson plans, observational logs, should all be typewritten.

As mentioned in an earlier chapter, students often want to keep handouts of articles and other resource materials distributed by professors. This portfolio is to showcase your work. If you have an article or piece of research that is connected to your philosophy, and the understandings gained from it are important to who you are as a teacher, you may keep it in your portfolio. You may do this only if it is accompanied by a reflective piece of writing that articulates what you have learned from it and why it is important to you as a teacher. If it is something you wish to keep for reference purposes, but not necessarily something that connects to your professionalism or your philosophy, keep it in an accordion file, or file folders, called "**Resources**".

In Chapter 2, you created a tentative Table of Contents, but it was general, based on the categories of your work. You will use it as a guide now, but you will probably tweak it if you change anything once your final artifact selections have been made. The following example uses the generic portfolio Table of Contents from Chapter 2, and has many of the subsections taken out, because the subsections will depend on your choices. The major sections have been left, because these are sections that will contain the body of your work that you should show to create a showcase that speaks to your teaching skills.

You will notice that the personal information is here, followed by a section for Child Development, Curriculum and Teaching, Special Coursework Projects, and Research Papers. The exams section is not considered essential in a showcase portfolio. I would only include it if the grades on exams were exemplary, or if your program required exam grades. If you are giving the showcase to a grad school, the grades they want to see are on your transcript. A showcase portfolio is more focused on your ability as a teacher, than on grades on exams in a particular course. You will be including transcripts to show course grades. Of course, you may want to keep notification on passing certification exams, but they will be in the Personal Section, or the Professional Development Section.

## Table of Contents

**Section 1. Introductory Material**

Personal Data (Name, Telephone Number, E-mail Address)

Portfolio Statement of Purpose

Professional Goals Statement

Resume

Letters of Recommendation

Autobiography

Teaching Philosophy

Transcripts

Video of You Teaching

**Section 2. Child Development**

(Papers on play, child development theory, room arrangement, etc.)

**Section 3. Assessment**

(Child Studies, observational records, children's work)

**Section 4. Curriculum and Teaching (Lesson Plans, Unit Plans, Curriculum Projects)**

**Section 5. Related Specialized Coursework Projects**

**Section 6. Research Papers**

**Section 7. Professional Development**

Certificates and Special Training

Institutes

Internships and Student Teaching

Logs

Time Sheets

If you want to arrange your portfolio according to the NAEYC Standards, you can use the following Table of Contents. Here you will be placing artifacts into the categories required by those standards. You could, if you so choose, create sections based on the INTASC Standards as well.

## PORTFOLIO

## Table of Contents

**Introductory Information**

      Personal Data (Name, Telephone, E-mail Address)

      Portfolio Statement of Purpose

      Goals Statement

      Resume

      Letters of Recommendation

      Autobiography

      Teaching Philosophy

      Transcripts

      Honors

**Section 1. Standard 1. Promoting Child Development and Learning**

      Research Papers on Child Development and Learning

      Projects on Play

      Projects on Room Arrangement

**Section 2. Standard 2. Building Family and Community Relationships**

      Research and Projects on Parent Involvement

      Research Projects on Community Relationships

**Section 3. Standard 3. Observing, Documenting, and Assessing, to Support Young Children and Families**

      Child Studies

**Section 4. Standard 4. Using Developmentally Effective Approaches to Connect with Children and Families**

**Section 5. Standard 5. Using Content Knowledge to Build Meaningful**

      Curriculum

      Unit Plans

      Videos of Lessons

      Evidence of Children's Work

      Reflections on Lessons

**Standard 6. Becoming a Professional**

      Certificates

      Workshops and Conferences

| PORTFOLIO |
|---|
| **Table of Contents (con't)** |
| Internships and Student Teaching |
| Logs |
| Time Sheets |

After you have tweaked the Portfolio Purpose Statement, Professional Goals Statement, Resume, Autobiography, and Teaching Philosophy, to reflect the picture of you, you can place those pieces in plastic sleeves and place them into your portfolio. Any certificates such as your Child Abuse and Neglect Certificate, First Aid, Violence Prevention, CDA, or any other certificate or honor that you have received should be placed into the portfolio. After the introductory material, you can begin to choose artifacts for the body of your portfolio. You can use the following Index Sheet, to keep track of the artifacts you include, and the standards you are addressing. You can begin by checking off the introductory material beginning with the tentative Table of Contents. If there is no change of sections in the portfolio from now until its completion, the Table of Contents will remain the same. If you should add a section, you can revise it. The Portfolio Index Sheet is intended to help you keep track of the work you have completed on your portfolio.

| Artifact | Entered Check | Rationale Draft/ Completed | Standard or Competency |
|---|---|---|---|
| | | | |

The heading of each column is related to the artifacts that you will be including. The Index Sheet at the end of the chapter lists the introductory material for you. You simply have to check off the introductory artifacts as you place them in the binder. There is no need for a rationale sheet for this introductory material, or for an entry into the standard or competency column. You will check off the "Rationale Drafted/ Completed" column, and the Standard or Competency column <u>only</u> for the artifacts of your work, such as your observations and lesson plans, and research papers.

## Connecting to the Competencies and Standards

As you select an artifact, you should be thinking about how your work meets the competencies and standards set by your program, certifying body, and the profession. The competencies expected by your program are typically found in the syllabi prepared by your professors and instructors. They tell you what skills and abilities they expect you to have learned by the completion of the course. You have also gleaned these competencies from the rubrics given for your performance on tasks assigned by your instructors and professors. Their comments and evaluations on your work are another indication of whether your work has met the competencies and standards that are set for your professional growth.

Your college program and/or certifying body has established the standards against which you should be measuring your work. We have provided the summaries of the NAEYC Standards and the website for a more detailed document of the standards in Chapter 2, on pps 19–23, and a website for the INTASC Standards in Chapter 4, on p. 44. Please Note: At the time of this book going to print, the INTASC Standards were in draft form waiting for public comment, and so could not be quoted as revisions might be made by the time of publication. These lists of the standards are summaries, because the list contains only the standards themselves. In the standards documents, the issuing bodies explain what the work that meets the standards looks like. They describe the characteristics of the work, and the kinds of work and teacher dispositions that meet the standards. By this stage of your growth, you might not need an explanation of the standards, but if you want a rich set of examples of work that meets the standards, you can consult the actual standards documents.

## Assembling the Portfolio

Next, you will assemble the artifacts that are the body of your work. Chapter 4 discussed the Rationale Test for helping you decide whether an artifact was a good choice, and for writing the rationale statements for each one. There are two examples on the process you would use for choosing an artifact and writing a rationale statement on a child study for a showcase portfolio. There is also one for a curriculum unit in Chapter 4, pp. 52, and 53–54 respectively.

The next pages discuss two other teaching examples that a student might include in a showcase portfolio. Included are sample rationale notes, and rationale statements, developed from the Rationale Test. Here is the test against which you will assess your artifacts.

| RATIONALE TEST |
|---|
| Artifact _____ Date _____ In ____ Out ____ |
| Reason for Rejection_____ |
| **1** |
| 1. What is this artifact and what did you do to develop it? (What?) |
| **2** |
| 2. How does this artifact demonstrate my growth as a professional and how does it help me meet the standards? (So What?) |
| **3** |
| 3. How will I use what I have learned in the future? (Now What?) |

A third-year student interned at a science institution. She was responsible for working with a science educator on Saturday and afternoon classes for children and families at the Aquarium. In addition to her internship duties assisting the science educator, she had to develop a lesson plan based on the exhibits on which she was most responsible for assisting the science educator. She wrote reflective logs on the experience. She researched titles of developmentally appropriate books, Internet resources to use as an early childhood teacher to extend and expand on the information, and hands-on work done at the Aquarium.

## RATIONALE TEST

Artifact <u>Log and Reflections on the Aquarium</u> Date _____ In __x__ Out _____

Reason for Rejection _____

### 1

1. What is this artifact and what did you do to develop it? (What?)

This is a Reflective Internship Log of my experiences working at the Aquarium. It demonstrates my experience working with informal education institutions and incorporating the exhibits at those institutions into my teaching plans. The artifact shows my ability to research resources such as books, CDs, and websites, appropriate for early childhood primary grades to enrich my science teaching.

### 2

2. How does this artifact demonstrate my growth as a professional and how does it help me meet the Standards? (So What?)

This curriculum unit shows my ability to develop hands-on classroom lessons related to the use of a science institution based on the inquiry approach. These lessons engage children in using science process skills and science journaling.

NAEYC Standard 4. Using Developmentally Effective Approaches to Connect Children and Families. 4b. Using Developmentally Effective Strategies and Tools for Early Education.

Standard 5. Using Content Knowledge for Building a Meaningful Curriculum. My lessons show child-centered approaches to science process skills, and the exploration of science content using strategies such as science journals, inquiry-based worksheets for data collection, and books, magazines, and websites for children's research supporting the growth of individual children and diversity of the group.

3. How will I use what I have learned in the future? (Now What?)

I will use science institutions and museums in my science and social studies teaching forever. I value the way these institutions make curriculum come alive for children by giving them hands-on experience with curriculum. I now volunteer at the Aquarium and intend to make it part of my life's work along with teaching. I hope to get my masters in science education and perhaps become a science cluster teacher to help children to love science.

When the student looks at her notes, it is clear that this set of artifacts is a good choice for her portfolio. It shows her abilities: researching resources for content learning and working with informal education institutions. It demonstrates her knowledge of science methodology and the inquiry approach, science process skills, and using science journals. She meets NAEYC Standards 4a, b, c, and d, and 5, because the activities that she created, and the resources she researched, are evidence of her creating developmentally appropriate curriculum that appeals to children with a variety of interests and abilities. The curriculum she constructed was based in inquiry, and was meaningful and challenging, engaging children in research, inquiry, and journaling. She also has found a commitment to science education that is a lifelong goal shown through her volunteer service, and her goals: a master's degree and a position as a science cluster teacher.

Therefore, this set of artifacts is one that she will choose for her portfolio. On the Rationale Test sheet, the student would check "In," because this is an artifact she is choosing. If it was an artifact that she did not think demonstrated significant work as a teacher, or growth as a professional, or move her closer to the standards and provide some significant growth as a professional, then she would check "Out" on the top of the sheet. She should then give a brief reason for rejecting this work. This note is important, because sometimes you reject a piece of work, and if no notation is made when you see it again, you have to go through the entire analytical process to identify the reason you did not want to use it. This is time consuming. So if you make a brief note here, and attach this Rationale Test sheet to the artifact, you will know why you decided to leave this material out of the portfolio.

## Writing the Rationale

The next step after choosing the artifact is to use the notes in the rationale sheet to write the rationale statement. Your rationale statement must reflect your voice and point of view. When we say your voice, we mean that you should authentically express the statement. As you write, you should be mindful of expressing who you are as a teacher while you are also giving information on the particular artifact that you are presenting. The rationale statement that you might write, based on the notes in the Rationale Test follows. Remember, as was stated earlier in the book and in this chapter, the readers of the showcase portfolio are usually pressed for time, so they are not likely to be able to read a long narrative rationale statement. Here you want to have brief, terse rationales that can be read quickly. You want the reader to get to your ideas quickly and, at the same time, to get a feeling for you and who you are.

## NOTES FROM THE RATIONALE TEST

This set of artifacts (lesson plans, annotated bibliography, and reflections) demonstrates my experience working with informal education institutions, and incorporating those exhibits into my teaching plans. The artifact shows my ability to research resources such as books, CDs, and websites, appropriate for early childhood primary grades, to enrich my science teaching.

This integrated curriculum unit shows my ability to develop hands-on classroom lessons, related to the use of a science institution based on the inquiry approach that engages children in using science process skills, and science journaling. I became so interested in this topic that I took the initiative to develop an annotated group of teaching resources for primary school teachers. My bibliography was incorporated into the resources of the Aquarium and is now distributed to teachers.

My work addresses NAEYC Standard 4. Using Developmentally Effective Approaches to Connect Children and Families. 4b. Using developmentally effective strategies and tools for early education. It also addresses Standard 5. Using Content Knowledge Building Meaningful Curriculum. My lessons show child-centered approaches to science process skills, and exploring science content using strategies such as science journals, inquiry-based worksheets for data collection, and use of science content books, magazines, and websites for children's research supporting the growth of individual children and the diversity of the group.

I will use science institutions and museums in my science and social studies teaching forever. I value the way these institutions make curriculum come alive for children, as well as giving them hands-on experience with curriculum. I now volunteer at the Aquarium and intend to make it my part of my life's work along with teaching. I hope to get my masters in science education and perhaps become a science cluster teacher to help children love science.

You will recall that at the beginning of this chapter, it was suggested that you reacquaint yourself with your Teaching Philosophy and your goals. You were encouraged to find your passions and interests. Now is the time that those things that set you apart should shine. You want the reader to focus on the important parts of these notes, and why this unit is important to you and to your showcase. You should edit and pare down the language to the main points you want to make. You should also consider giving the Rationale Statement a title, which sets the stage for the artifacts and gives the reader a sense of why you think the work is significant to you as a teacher and to the profession. The edited version of the Rationale Statement with a title follows.

---

### NOTES FROM THE RATIONALE TEST

**Discovering a Love for Science: My Internship and Inquiry at the Aquarium**

This group of artifacts includes:

- Logs and reflections on my work interning at the New York Aquarium;

- Lesson plans based on exhibits;

- An annotated bibliography I created of science content books, CDs, and websites for early childhood education.

My internship at the New York Aquarium helped me discover a love for science education that is now becoming a lifelong teaching goal. These artifacts demonstrate my experience working with informal education institutions, and incorporating the exhibits at those institutions into my teaching plans. The artifacts show my initiative and ability to research resources such as books, CDs, and websites appropriate for early childhood primary grades, to enrich my science teaching. My bibliography was incorporated into the resources of the Aquarium and is now distributed to teachers.

My curriculum unit shows my ability to develop hands-on lessons based on the inquiry approach that engages children in using science process skills, and science journaling, inquiry-based worksheets for data collection, and age-appropriate science content books, magazines, and websites for children's research, that supports the growth of individual children and the group. These approaches meet NAEYC Standard 4. Using Developmentally Effective Approaches to Connect Children and Families; Standard 5. Using Content Knowledge Building Meaningful Curriculum.

This experience has taught me the value of using science institutions and museums in my science and social studies teaching. I value the way these institutions make curriculum come alive for children giving them hands-on experience with curriculum, and I will use them throughout my career. I now volunteer at the Aquarium, and intend along with teaching, to make it my part of my life's work. I now plan to get my masters in science education and become a science cluster teacher, so as to help children love science.

You can block text and place it so that the ideas stand out, by using PowerPoint. PowerPoint will also allow you to add clip art, photographs, background formatting, and borders.

# Discovering a Love for Science: My Internship and Inquiry at the Aquarium

This group of artifacts includes:

Logs and reflections on my work as an intern at the New York Aquarium;

Lesson plans based on exhibits;

An annotated bibliography, which I created, of science content books, CD's, and internet sites for early childhood education.

My internship at the New York Aquarium helped me discover a love for science education that is now becoming a life long teaching goal. These artifacts demonstrate my experience working with informal education institutions and incorporating the exhibits at those institutions into my teaching plans. The artifacts show my initiative and ability to research resources such as books, CD's and Internet websites, appropriate for early childhood primary grades, to enrich my science teaching. My bibliography was incorporated into the resources of the Aquarium, and is now distributed to teachers.

**Example of Slide for Reflective log on Internship**

**How will I use this in the future?**

**This internship changed my career goals…**
- This experience has taught me the value of using science institutions, and museums in my science and social studies teaching. I value the way these institutions make curriculum come alive for children by giving them hands-on experience with curriculum, and will use them throughout my career. I now volunteer at the Aquarium and along with teaching, plan to make it part of my life's work. I now plan to get my masters in science education and become a science cluster teacher to help children love science.

**Reflection on Internship Log cont'd**

My curriculum unit shows my ability to develop hands-on classroom lessons, based on the inquiry approach, which engage children in using science process skills, and science journaling. My lessons show child centered approaches to science teaching, engaging children in science process skills, and exploring science content, using strategies such as science journals, inquiry-based work sheets for data collection, and use of age appropriate science content books, magazines, and websites for children's research, supporting the growth of indivtdual children and the group. These approaches meet the NAEYC Standard 4. Using Developmentally Effective Approaches to Connect Children and Families, 4a, b, c, and d; and Standard 5 Using Content Knowledge Building Meaningful Curriculum, 5a, 5b, and 5c, INTASC Standard 1. Knowledge of Subject Matter.

**Reflection on Internship Log and the Standards**

Here is one more example of student work with sample Rationale Notes and Rationale Statement.

A third-year student who took a course in the Child, Family and Community, did a project on the issue of parent involvement at a Universal Pre-kindergarten program. After interviewing the teacher and parents she was made aware of the parents' lack of understanding about why children were engaged in play. They wanted to see worksheets, and more academic skill sheets sent home. The student observed, at a parent workshop, that parents did respond to the teacher's explanation for the play activities. She developed a newsletter that showcased children's work, with brief commentary about what skills children were learning. Her artifacts consist of reflective logs about the experience, a final evaluative report, the actual newsletters, the cooperating teacher evaluations, and parents' comments.

## RATIONALE TEST

Artifact __ Parent Involvement Project _ UPK Date _____ In _x ____ Out _____

Reason for Rejection _____

### 1. What is this artifact and what did you do to develop it? (What?)

This is a parent newsletter that I created to share information on play and learning with UPK parents. I worked with the early childhood team (assistant teacher, teacher, and parents) to develop and distribute it.

### 2. How does this artifact demonstrate my growth as a professional and help me meet the standards? (So What?)

I was able to investigate an important issue, collect information on different sides of an issue, reflect, and come up with a solution.

It demonstrates that I am able to build a relationship between school and home, and empower parents with information that helps children grow and develop. I am creative, I problem solve, and I persevere.

Standard 2. Building Family and Community Relationships, because my newsletter gave parents information about child development and how children learn.

### 3. How will I use what I have learned in the future? (Now What?)

I will look for a variety of ways to communicate and work better with parents and family members to help support children.

The student took the notes and wrote them out in narrative form and edited them. The statement follows.

---

**SAMPLE RATIONALE**

**Creating a UPK Newsletter and Parent and School Communication**

The artifacts found here are:

A Case Study of Parent Involvement at a UPK Program

Reflective Logs and Final Report

Teacher Evaluation and Evaluations of Parents

Two UPK Newsletters

I created and distributed a UPK Newsletter for Parents at _____ UPK. This work includes my case study of this project and shows my ability to create a way to communicate with parents about child development and how children learn. I gathered information through interviews with the teacher, teacher assistant, and parents. The newsletter I created highlighted children's work, and gave tips about how to follow up at home. Parents then told us anecdotes of their activities, which we included in the next issue. This activity fostered two-way communication between the program and home. It also empowered parents with information on child development, to support their children's growth and development.

The project showed my work toward NAEYC Standard 2. Building Family and Community Relationships, because the project developed communication between parents and the UPK Program.

**I believe that when parents and teachers work together, children learn better.**

This project has taught me the importance of parent–teacher communication and cooperation, which I hope to make a major part of my role as a teacher, through parent workshops, newsletters, and conferences.

---

Here is the rationale blocked, using PowerPoint including a piece of clip art that is illustrative of the topic. If this student prefers, she might scan and insert a piece of artwork or the cover from her own newsletter.

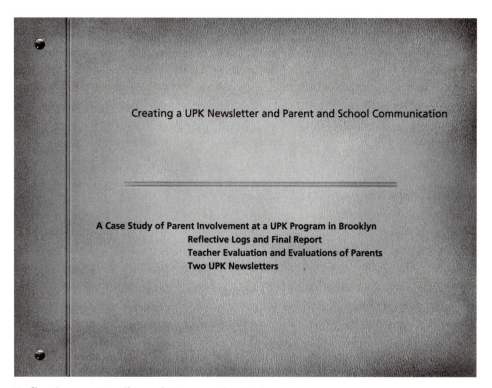

Creating a UPK Newsletter and Parent and School Communication

A Case Study of Parent Involvement at a UPK Program in Brooklyn
Reflective Logs and Final Report
Teacher Evaluation and Evaluations of Parents
Two UPK Newsletters

**Reflection on Family and Community Project**

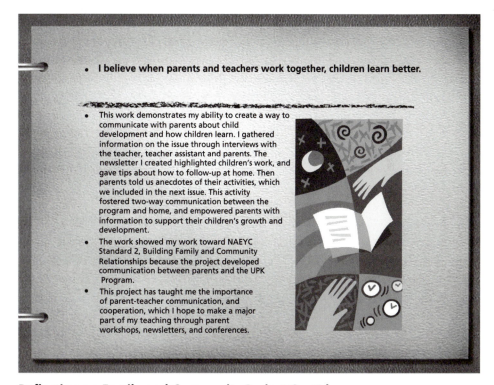

- I believe when parents and teachers work together, children learn better.

- This work demonstrates my ability to create a way to communicate with parents about child development and how children learn. I gathered information on the issue through interviews with the teacher, teacher assistant and parents. The newsletter I created highlighted children's work, and gave tips about how to follow-up at home. Then parents told us anecdotes of their activities, which we included in the next issue. This activity fostered two-way communication between the program and home, and empowered parents with information to support their children's growth and development.

- The work showed my work toward NAEYC Standard 2, Building Family and Community Relationships because the project developed communication between parents and the UPK Program.

- This project has taught me the importance of parent-teacher communication, and cooperation, which I hope to make a major part of my teaching through parent workshops, newsletters, and conferences.

**Reflection on Family and Community Project Cont'd**

Now it is your turn to look at your artifacts and identify pieces of work that give a comprehensive portrait of you as a teacher.

1. Test your artifacts using the Rationale Test.

2. If the artifact is a good choice, use the notes to draft a Rationale Statement.

3. Edit the Rationale Statement.

One by one, you can look at each piece of work and ask, "Does it help show my development, and represent my goals and/or my abilities, as a teacher?" Then, for any piece that you think fits that picture, use the Rationale Test. By applying that test, you will arrive at those things you have learned, the standards you have tried to meet, and what you will take with you into the future.

## Prepare for Presentation

All of your work should be professionally presented. Now that you know the work you will be presenting, it will be easier to add finishing touches to your presentation that will show your work in the best professional light.

You should have Rationale Statements for each artifact, or group of artifacts, that you wish to include in the portfolio. Be sure you have proofread your rationale statement for proper grammar and spelling. Give the Rationale Statement a title (e.g., Rationale Statement for **Reflection on a Visit to Montessori School**), and give it whatever formatting your college program requires. If there is none, you can use the following generic format.

---

June __, 20__

Rationale Statement for

"Reflection on a Visit to Montessori School"

By Jane Doe

NAEYC Standards Addressed 1, and 4b

*[The Rationale statement goes here.]*

---

If you use a formatting program such as PowerPoint, you are presented with templates that make the formatting easier and more professional-looking. To add interest, you can select a background, and/or select a piece of clip art or a photo that can be illustrative of the artifact's topic. Give the rationale a title and/or bold important elements, so that the main ideas stand out. Next, you will see that version of the last rationale on Parent Involvement on page 105.

Software programs such as Microsoft Word and PowerPoint provide the availability of a variety of fonts, patterns for creating block print, arched designs, clip art, and many other graphic design features that students might sometimes want to use to decorate their document's cover pages with some graphic design. If you have stored your own digital photographs on your computer, you can use them to decorate your work as well. Just as was suggested for the Developmental portfolio, here in your Showcase portfolio you focus first on the content of your work rather than many "bells and whistles" on the cover or to decorate the rationale statements. Keep your design ideas simple and consistent. If you put a border on your rationale page, use it for all of the rationale sheets so that there is a consistency in the document. If you select an icon or graphic image to signify a particular category of artifact, or a particular kind of document, try to have it complement the work, not detract from it. The graphic should not be the focus of attention. Your work, and your ideas about teaching and learning, should be the focus. Principals, directors, and professors are interested in your ideas about child development and teaching, not in how many clip art pictures you can access. So keep it simple.

Place the Rationale Sheet in a plastic sleeve, and insert the artifact in its own plastic sleeve(s). Place them in the appropriate section in your binder. Although it may have taken awhile to learn this process, once you understand it, your work should go quickly. However, do not take short cuts on the care you put into it and your attention to detail, just to do it quickly. Take care to do it well.

Once you place the document in the portfolio, write its name into the Artifact Index Sheet. List the name of the artifact, the date you entered it, check off whether the Rationale is a draft, or completed, and the Standard or Competency the artifact relates to. The purpose of these notations is to help you keep track of where you are in your work, and to organize the process. Sometimes you are working on the portfolio and need to stop. If you quickly note where you are with an artifact, you won't have to redo the work and the analysis to get up to speed when you begin again.

# Artifact Index Sheet

| Artifact | Entered Check | Rationale Draft/Completed | Standard or Competency |
|---|---|---|---|
| Table of Contents | | | |
| Purpose Statement | | | |
| Personal Goals Statement | | | |
| Resume | | | |
| Autobiography | | | |
| Teaching Philosophy | | | |
| Teaching Video | | | |
| Certificates and Honors | | | |
| | | | |
| | | | |
| Transcript(s) | | | |
| | | | |
| | | | |
| Letters of Recommendation | | | |
| | | | |
| | | | |
| Child Development (Papers on child development theory, play, observations, child studies) | | | |
| | | | |
| | | | |
| | | | |
| | | | |
| Curriculum and Teaching (Lesson Plans, Unit Plans, Curriculum Projects) | | | |
| | | | |
| | | | |
| | | | |
| | | | |
| | | | |
| Related Specialized Coursework Projects (Family and Community, Psychology, Special Education, Speech and Language) | | | |
| | | | |
| | | | |
| | | | |
| | | | |
| Research Papers | | | |
| | | | |
| | | | |
| | | | |
| | | | |
| | | | |

## Artifact Index Sheet (con't)

| Artifact | Entered Check | Rationale Draft/Completed | Standard or Competency |
|---|---|---|---|
| Exams | | | |
| | | | |
| | | | |
| | | | |
| | | | |
| Professional Development (workshops, certificates, memberships in professional organizations) | | | |
| | | | |
| | | | |
| Miscellaneous | | | |
| | | | |
| | | | |
| | | | |

If you would prefer to use an Index sheet organized according to the NAEYC Standards, you can find a downloadable version online on our website.

Next you will assemble the artifacts that are the body of your work.

### Preparing a Cover Page

You will want to develop a cover page. You did not prepare a cover page at the beginning of the process, because when you began, your picture of yourself and your portfolio was incomplete. You were still constructing it. Now you know who you are as a teacher, and you have the portrait you wanted to build. At this point, all you need to do is find the proper frame for it. You must now design a cover page, and give it a title that represents you. You can use Microsoft Word or PowerPoint. If you use Word, you will notice that under "Insert menu," you can insert clip art, photos, Word Art (text in different designs). You can design a cover page that represents you. Here is an example of a page using PowerPoint.

# My Early Childhood Teaching Portfolio

## Showcasing:

### Unit and Lesson Plans

### Child Studies

### Research Papers

#### By Jenny Vasquez

**Cover page example for a Showcase Portfolio**

## Concluding Remarks

In this chapter, you built your showcase portfolio. As you created your showcase portfolio, you constructed the story of who you are as a teacher. The reflection you did on your work helped you construct knowledge about yourself, and your growth into the teacher you are today. The work you did should help to remind you of why you decided to become a teacher. You may have become reacquainted with the milestones in your development that shaped your values and beliefs. You reconnected with the theory and good practices that formed your foundation as a professional, and you refined and tweaked your Autobiography and Teaching Philosophy. You collected groups of work to reflect a comprehensive picture of you as one who understands child development, assessment, and teaching and learning. The work you did in organizing and building this portfolio should enable you to see how all of your study helped to develop the teacher you have become. You have also developed a cover page that presents your work to the public. All of the work done in this chapter will help you to showcase your accomplishments and develop a portrait of who you are as a teacher. It will also help to tell the story of what you know. The nuances of this portrait are wrought by the rationales you have crafted, which give the reader of your portfolio a window into your thinking about teaching and learning, and your belief system about the profession.

This is a major accomplishment. It has taken you two or four, or more, years to develop this body of work, as well as to select just the right comprehensive groups of work to showcase your talents and abilities as a teacher. Take some time to absorb the experiences and growth that this portfolio represents.

## What You Have Accomplished in This Chapter

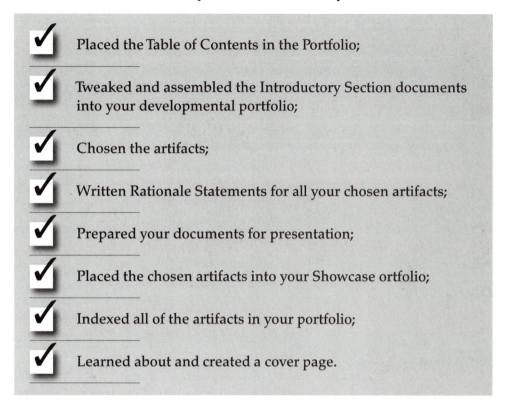

✔ Placed the Table of Contents in the Portfolio;

✔ Tweaked and assembled the Introductory Section documents into your developmental portfolio;

✔ Chosen the artifacts;

✔ Written Rationale Statements for all your chosen artifacts;

✔ Prepared your documents for presentation;

✔ Placed the chosen artifacts into your Showcase ortfolio;

✔ Indexed all of the artifacts in your portfolio;

✔ Learned about and created a cover page.

# The e-Portfolio

In this chapter, you will learn about e-portfolios, and how this form of portfolio might be an option for you. In Chapters 5 and 6, we talked about creating a developmental portfolio, and a showcase portfolio. Either kind of portfolio can be made as an e-portfolio. Dr. Helen Barrett, a respected leader in research and spokesperson in the field of e-portfolios, defines e-portfolios like this:

> An **electronic portfolio** uses electronic technologies, allowing the portfolio developer to collect and organize portfolio artifacts in many media types (audio, video, graphics, text). A standards-based portfolio uses a database or hypertext links to clearly show the relationship between the standards or goals, artifacts and reflections. The learner's reflections are the rationale that specific artifacts are evidence of achieving the stated standards or goals. . . . An electronic portfolio is not a haphazard collection of artifacts (i.e., a digital scrapbook or a multimedia presentation) but rather a reflective tool that demonstrates growth over time.
>
> (Barrett, 2000)

An e-portfolio is basically a digital record of the artifacts and rationales for your work, which is preserved on a DVD or stored on a server for viewing on the Internet. Because you are using a computer and software to collect and organize your e-portfolio, you can hyperlink the standards that you refer to in your rationales and reflections strengthening your presentation of your work. Anything that you can store in your binder portfolio, you can store in an e-portfolio. Your lesson plans, observations, and reflective writings are stored as word processing documents. They can be uploaded to, and stored in, a server, or on CD or DVD. You can scan student work and documents such as certificates, and store the digital images in an e-portfolio.

Some things that are not so easy to store in a binder are more easily stored and accessed through an e-Portfolio. Video clips of your teaching can be stored in an e-portfolio, as can digital photos of children at work, and digital pictures of bulletin board displays of work children did under your supervision. In addition, you can include links to standards, or to websites, that demonstrate how you would use the Internet in your teaching. The e-portfolio is a very dynamic tool for students and professionals, because it allows you to create a portfolio that can be widely accessible, and that you can develop and change over time, so that it displays your growing skills and abilities as a teacher, as well as your knowledge of technology.

The National Council for the Accreditation of Teacher Education (NCATE) has incorporated the need for technology education for pre-service teachers into the standards set for institutions, that prepare teachers. NCATE suggests that one way for teachers to become knowledgeable about technology is to practice those skills developing an e-portfolio. Through pre-service teachers' exploration of technology skills, they will gain the skills they should be teaching children to become technologically literate. The International Society for Technology in Education (ISTE) project, the National Educational Technology for Students (NETS) has developed standards for Pre-K through 12 in technology education. The project standards document, "National Educational Technology Standards for Students: The Next Generation" lists a variety of abilities that children should have if they are to function, create, and be contributing citizens in today's technology and information age. Here is a summary of the standards that the project says: "What students should know and be able to do to learn effectively and live productively in an increasingly digital world . . ."

### 1. Creativity and Innovation

Students demonstrate creative thinking, construct knowledge, and develop innovative products and processes using technology.

### 2. Communication and Collaboration

Students use digital media and environments to communicate and work collaboratively, including at a distance, to support individual learning and contribute to the learning of others.

### 3. Research and Information Fluency

Students apply digital tools to gather, evaluate, and use information.

### 4. Critical Thinking, Problem-Solving & Decision-Making

Students use critical thinking skills to plan and conduct research, manage projects, solve problems and make informed decisions using appropriate digital tools and resources.

### 5. Digital Citizenship

Students understand human, cultural, and societal issues related to technology and practice legal and ethical behavior.

### 6. Technology Operations and Concepts

Students demonstrate a sound understanding of technology concepts, systems and operations.

Here is a link to a full description of those standards that have been generally agreed upon by professional associations of teachers, principals, and school superintendents as important for children Pre-K to 12 to have:

http://www.iste.org/inhouse/nets/cnets/students/pdf/NETS_for_Students_2007.pdf

Here is the website of the National Educational Technology for Students

http://cnets.iste.org/

where you can learn more about technology education.

## Advantages and Disadvantages of e-Portfolio

There are advantages and disadvantages to creating an e-portfolio. Knowing the advantages and disadvantages is important, because it will prepare you for the work ahead if you should choose to develop an e-portfolio. But it will also let you know about what you have to look forward to, as the process gets under way.

The advantages of developing an e-portfolio are the skills and abilities teachers will learn, and the ways in which they will be able to support the growth of children in the early childhood grades. The advantages are also connected to the accessibility, availability, and dynamic nature of the e-portfolio.

### Constructing Knowledge about Technology

Early childhood teachers believe in constructing knowledge and experiential learning. One major advantage of creating an e-portfolio is that as you are learning to construct your portfolio by putting into practice skills and abilities using technology and the Internet. You are also learning the technological skills that the profession now agrees are important to teaching. Many of the skills that you acquire can be passed on to children. You can teach them to gather information, research topics, access data, and create reports using today's tools: the computer and the Internet. If you love technology and have already engaged in social networking and uploading digital images, you might enjoy playing in this media. You will learn how to:

- make hyperlinks to your work or to documents on the Internet;
- illustrate your work with images and sound;
- upload videos of your teaching.

Learning new skills to add to your technical understandings will be fun and make you feel good about your ability to build a website that represents you as a professional.

### Supporting Lifelong Learning in Today's World

Teachers have always given children the skills and abilities to read and write and compute, but we have noted that it is not enough to teach skills without inculcating values such as valuing lifelong learning. As early childhood educators, we speak about helping children to learn how to learn, and to enjoy the challenge of learning. The world we live in is information-driven. Never before have student-centered values, such as lifelong learning, and the disposition of being self-motivated and wanting to learn, been more needed. Children need the technological tools to become lifelong learners, and to problem solve, and to learn independently, as well as cooperatively with others. As their teachers, we must give them those tools. One way to learn what we need to teach them is to begin learning the technology yourself. So, as you construct knowledge about developing this e-portfolio, you will be developing skills that will help you to raise the technological literacy of your future students.

### Demonstrating Your Skills to Others

An added advantage is that you will be demonstrating these abilities to your professors, principals, directors, and other viewers of your portfolio. As they navigate your e-portfolio, they will become aware of your abilities to use the computer not only for word processing, but uploading documents, graphically designing a web page, and uploading digital photos, video, and audio. You will also be able to demonstrate your ability to include links to other websites, and to navigate the web. These abilities will give you an advantage over other candidates for teaching positions, and will demonstrate your own commitment to keeping professionally current and prepared for today's teaching challenges.

### e-Portfolios Are Accessible

Another advantage of the e-portfolio is that it is easily accessible. Whether your e-portfolio is stored on a CD or DVD or in a server at an e-portfolio service, your work is available to your audience, without your having to hand-deliver a large bulky binder. The CD or DVD can be mailed to a principal or to a director. The person whom you wish to see your portfolio can be an invited guest, and given access to your portfolio at your e-portfolio service on the Internet. If your site is published on the web and open to the public, all you need do is e-mail the web address or URL to the people you wish to see your e-portfolio. Most services are accessible 24 hours a day. Anywhere that a guest has a computer, at any time of the day, he or she can view your portfolio. When the material is web-based, it is accessible anywhere in the world where web access exists.

### Accessibility Promotes Dialogue and Collaboration

The accessibility of the e-portfolios has created another advantage in that it promotes a dialogue between teacher and students, and discussion among students. E-Portfolio software can store projects that college professors or instructors assign, and students can grant them access to the work for commentary. Rubrics for the work can be stored, and can provide the students a means of soliciting feedback, and a framework for assessing their work. The rubrics, comments, peer feedback, and the actual work can all be stored. Students collaborating on a project can share and collect their work, and give each other access to the work being stored on the server. They may view each other's submission, and dialogue about changes, additions, and improvements that they might wish to make.

### e-Portfolios Are Dynamic

Because the e-portfolio is computer-built, it has a dynamic nature that the binder does not have. If you are near a computer, you can update documents, upload changes, and have your portfolio grow and change as you grow and change. You can create more than one version of your e-portfolio, so that it suits the particular audience, in which you are interested. You may wish to keep both a developmental e-portfolio, and a showcase e-portfolio. You may want to showcase two different aspects of your work, for different potential employers. For example, you might have a portfolio with a focus on science education for a science cluster teacher position, and a generalist version for a job as a first-grade teacher. You might have a version for graduate schools more focused on teaching and your research.

## The Disadvantages

The disadvantages are few, but they are worth recognizing because knowing them in advance will help you to easily overcome any challenges they may present.

### Learning to Use Technology Takes Time

One major disadvantage of electronic portfolios is, that if you are not technologically literate, you will have to learn how to use the equipment and programs that support the work that you will have to do. Learning these technologies takes time. You will, therefore, have to devote the time and effort to learning the new skills and abilities that you will be using as you construct your portfolio. Even though more and more colleges are adopting e-portfolios, you may be one of the first students at your college to explore the process. There may not be as many students, at your college, who have the experience to help mentor you through the process. As a result, you will have to rely on the portfolio service the college has engaged for technical advice, or the computer tech people at your college. Until you become proficient with the programs and the processes, learning to use the e-portfolio, may be challenging and a bit frustrating.

### Focus on Technology Can Make You Lose Focus on the Work and the Reflection

Another disadvantage is that it is easy to focus on the technology, and lose focus on the substance of the portfolio, the artifacts and your reflective thinking, which are what the work is about. One way to avoid this is to reflect on your work, using tools with which you are most comfortable. Some students are more open to reflecting in their own handwriting in a notebook or a journal. Others have become comfortable writing reflectively on the computer. What is essential is to reflect in a way that helps you to learn about yourself as a teacher. Then you can take those ideas and insights you have about yourself as a teacher, and type it into a word processing document. You should focus on teaching and learning first, and then on how to design and construct the technology.

Where should you begin? The first thing to do is to explore a bit, and see what other teaching e-portfolios look like. Dr. Helen Barrett, a major figure in the research about e-portfolios, keeps a site that has a wide variety of e-portfolios for many different purposes. You can find some pre-service teacher e-portfolios on the web at the following sites:

http://electronicportfolios.com/examples/index.html
http://electronicportfolios.org/teachers/index.html

There are sites devoted to e-portfolios and learning about the process of constructing one.

If you use a search engine, you can find additional examples by searching for "teacher e-portfolios examples." By exploring a few, you will see the variety of portfolios that reflect the students and teachers who have prepared them. E-portfolios are not limited to teaching because the web is used for showcasing yourself in a variety of professions, so there are e-portfolios created by students in any number of fields. There are e-portfolios created by professors and those created by institutions. Here are some sites available to students in colleges and institutions. Here is one at La Guardia Community College of the City University of New York.

http://www.eportfolio.lagcc.cuny.edu/

The state of Minnesota has provided e-portfolio services for all of its residents.

http://www.efoliominnesota.com/

They say on their site, "Welcome to eFolio Minnesota, a multimedia electronic portfolio designed to help you create a living showcase of your education, career and personal achievements. All Minnesota residents, including students enrolled in Minnesota schools, educators and others can use eFolio Minnesota to reach their career and education goals."
You can see that educational institutions, and a variety of entities are all supporting the education and development of students and people in the workforce to learn and use this powerful new tool.

Explore a few sites and discover some of the features of the e-portfolio. This Reflective Task Sheet will guide you as you explore and learn.

## Reflection on e-Portfolio

1. How do the e-portfolio creators capture your interest and give you a first impression of them and their work? (Cite the website if you want to return to it.)

2. In the teaching portfolios, how do the different students bring attention to their work (artifacts such as lesson plans and observations)?

3. In the teaching portfolios, how is the work organized? Did they use standards as an organizational tool?

4. Do you notice any common features of the e-portfolios that you saw?

5. Were there any features that you liked and want to incorporate into your e-portfolio? Why? Cite the website.

6. Were there any features that you disliked and want to avoid in creating your e-portfolio? Why? Cite the website.

7. What have you learned from your exploration of e-portfolios that you will use in the future?

### Reflecting on the Process of Building an e-Portfolio

As an early childhood educator, you know the importance of experiential learning, and how gaining experience with a process will help you to gain the skills and abilities necessary to use it better. A major aspect of building an e-portfolio is developing slides from templates, which will contain the ideas, information, and images, that will portray you and your work to your viewer. If you gain some experience with the particular e-portfolio software, platform your college uses, or Microsoft PowerPoint, it will be easier to construct your portfolio than if you try to construct it while you are learning the process. So, explore the templates, and how to design text and backgrounds, how to add clip art and photos, and how to link to uploaded documents from your computer (e.g., lesson plans, observations, research papers). Play with the software and create an experimental e-portfolio document. After you have explored and experimented with the service or the program, reflect on the process and respond to the following questions.

1. As you explored the process used for building an e-portfolio, what did you enjoy most? Why?

2. What in the process caused you the most frustration or difficulty? Why?

3. What do you think you will gain from the process?

4. What challenges do you anticipate?

5. What resources are currently available to you to overcome the challenges you foresee? Be specific with the names and numbers of technical assistants, and web addresses for assistance.

6. How do you plan to overcome the challenges?

## Choose Your Artifacts

If you are creating a developmental portfolio, you can use the process for choosing artifacts and writing the rationales that you explored in Chapter 5. If you are creating a showcase portfolio, you can use the process found in Chapter 6. You can also use the instructions in the these chapters for connecting to the competencies, and writing your Rationale Statements. What will be different, as you construct the e-portfolio, is where you put your rationales and where you place your artifacts. Based on the fact that you will be placing this material in a template on a server, or on a template such as those in Microsoft

PowerPoint in preparation for a CD or DVD, you must consider a way to design your presentation.

The artifacts you choose should tell the story about your development or about who you are as a teacher today. What is distinctive about the e-portfolio is that this story will be experienced on the computer screen. Your attention, therefore, must be on both the content (what you say) and the media (the way it looks to the viewer).

## Important Note: Your e-Portfolio on the Web

There are major considerations that you must take into account, as you collect artifacts for your e-portfolio. As you think about the artifacts you exhibit, you must consider the public nature of the e-portfolio, especially if it is going to be viewed on the World Wide Web. Therefore, you need to be careful about what you place in the portfolio, and to be sure to specify who views the site. You also want to protect the images of children, and their names if you exhibit digital photos of them or their work.

If you are placing material on a portfolio service server, there will be a process for specifying who sees the material. There is usually a guest book of sorts or a list of preferences that allows you to designate guest viewers to whom you give access. You then might give the invited guest a password for easy entry into the site. You can protect your own site if you have it hosted on a server on your own. The server will tell you the steps to take if there is something on the site that requires privacy.

Some sites are open to the public and, therefore, it is your responsibility, as you choose artifacts, to select wisely. You might make sure that certain items are only available upon request after the viewer asks for permission to view them. Viewers, then, would have to contact you (usually by e-mail) for such permission, and you could determine whether you wanted to give them access. A resume might be protected that way if, for example, you did not want your entire job history on the web.

In Chapter 5 on the Developmental Portfolio, and Chapter 6 on the Showcase Portfolio, in the sections entitled, Important Note on Confidentiality and Protecting the Identity of Children, it was stated that confidentiality of children's records including their names and other identifiable characteristics of children must be protected. It bears repeating here. Any artifacts that you use in your portfolio that are related to children, **must not** include information that reveals their identity.

Here in the e-Portfolio it is essential that you do not want to make identifiable information available to anyone who might use it to prey upon children whose images you use on your site. So, if you upload children's work, take their names off their work or use only their first initial, or a pseudonym. The same is true in the case of any digital images of children at work on projects. When using photographs of children at work, you can also take care to use only those which focus on the work, rather than full portraits of the child(ren). If you videotape yourself teaching, video children only from the back. In other words, you can take pictures over the shoulders of children at work, so that one does not see their full faces. *Also, never put a child's name and school or identifying information on an e-portfolio.*

Lastly, but very important, is the issue of respecting the intellectual property of others. You cannot copy and use any one's digital photos, or artwork without permission. There are images on sites on the Internet that you are free to use, but they have a message to that effect on the site.

## Digitize Your e-Portfolio Artifacts

The first step in creating an e-portfolio is to digitize all of your portfolio artifacts by placing them onto the computer, and placing them into a folder named "e-Portfolio." Any documents that have already been written and saved on the computer, such as your lesson plans, essays, and observations, should be saved in your "e-Portfolio" file folder. If you did your rationale sheets in a word processing document, place them in the folder as well. Any artifacts such as digital photos should also be placed here. Anything that is hard copy (paper) should be scanned into the computer (copies of certificates). If you do not have a scanner, use the scanner in the college technology center. There are also scanners in most copy center stores, where you pay a fee for use of the equipment based on the time used. You should scan them and place the images in your "e-Portfolio" file. You can also take digital pictures of pieces of children's work, bulletin board displays, charts or graphs made during your lessons, and so on.

Next, organize the documents in this e-portfolio file folder. One simple plan of organization is to divide the work into two folders within the e-portfolio folder:

1. About You;

2. About Your Work.

The material "About You" will contain all of the introductory documents including your Portfolio Goals Statement, Autobiography, Teaching Philosophy, Resume, and Professional Goals. Your artifacts or actual work can be placed in the second folder. If you have many artifacts and their corresponding Rationale Statements, you will want to keep them organized. You can organize your work according to the standards. You can put six folders in the "My Work" folder naming them "Standard 1," "Standard 2," "Standard 3," "Standard 4," "Standard 5," and "Standard 6." You can then place the work and Rationale Statements for each standard in its own folder. Your folders would look like this:

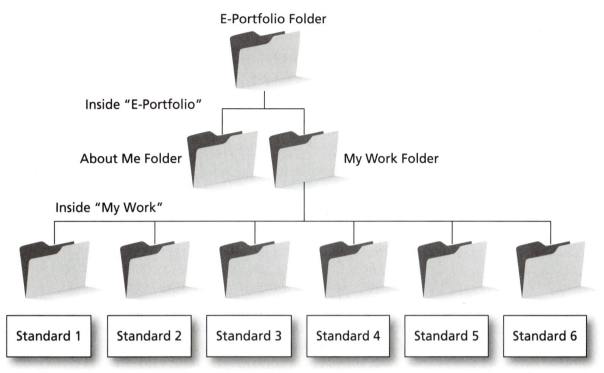

E-Portfolio Folder

Inside "E-Portfolio"

About Me Folder

My Work Folder

Inside "My Work"

| Standard 1 | Standard 2 | Standard 3 | Standard 4 | Standard 5 | Standard 6 |

**Example of the e-Portfolio Folders**

Think of putting your e-portfolio documents in these folders on your computer, as you would be doing if you were filing this material hard copy in manila file folders. If you do this now, when you begin to place something in the actual e-portfolio, you will be able to find it. Rather than searching through your entire documents-filled computer, you will go directly to the e-portfolio file folder and select your documents.

## Decide on Your Story

Because an e-portfolio is seen on a computer screen, and is a visual medium, you need to plan your story out like a movie. You should create a storyboard that is a pictorial representation of what you plan your presentation to look like. Designing your presentation is important because in a binder-type portfolio, your cover page invites the viewer to open the binder. The viewer uses the tabs and dividers and your Table of Contents as tools for finding information. He or she flips the pages or sections based on his interest. In an e-portfolio your computer screen presents a visual image, and the buttons or links you click are like the tabs. It is interactive because the buttons, when clicked, allow the viewer to flip through the portfolio "pages" and the links you create. So, you have to decide on your story, and the way in which you will organize the activity of your viewer(s), so that he or she can focus on you and your work, and is easily able to find artifacts and their rationales.

One way to begin is to sketch out a storyboard that will resemble the pathways you will create for your e-portfolio. It will be your plan for the placement of things and the order of their appearance in the portfolio.

If it has been a long time since you did the exploration of the various teacher portfolios and you cannot recall the ones you liked, revisit them. You may want to refresh your recollection of the program of templates that you are using as well. Microsoft PowerPoint is used here in this chapter to demonstrate an e-portfolio pages, as will screen shots of students actual e-portfolios made using Digication, an e-portfloio software. Now, you are ready to begin to create a storyboard for your e-portfolio.

## Create a Storyboard

The storyboard that you make will tell the story of your development as a teacher if it is a developmental e-portfolio, or it will tell the story of who you are as a teacher today if it is a showcase e-portfolio. The storyboard is your plan for laying out the visuals that your audience will see, and the plan for how they will access your images.

First you should design your welcome page. To do so you have to answer a few questions:

- What will it say?
- What images will it contain?
- How will it orient the viewer to go through your work?

You want your portfolio to welcome the viewer and give them a good first impression of you. You want them to know right away what kind of portfolio they are seeing. You also want to let them know how to navigate your portfolio in order to find the things that they want to see.

Most e-portfolios have a welcome page, and a series of buttons that you can click to navigate the portfolio. What you are doing as you design this page is organizing the path one will take to get to your work. The list of buttons are like the Table of Contents tabs on a paper binder. Here In Fig. 7-1a is an example of a welcome page with navigation buttons along the left side. Each e-portfolio platform or software has a template you can use to organize your welcome page. In this one, using Power Point, the student put the buttons along the left-hand side, and created an "About Me" section which has in it a page called "My Autobiography," a page called "My Portfolio Purpose Statement," My Teaching Philosophy," and "My Professional Goals." She has a second section called "About My Work and the NAEYC Standards." That second section has pages organized according to the standards, and will contain her work that relates to each standard.

You will notice on the plan for this presentation in Figure 1b, you can see a a sketch planning the Welcome Page, In the 7-1b, on the "Welcome" screen there is a button to click, which says "All About Me" that leads the viewer to the student's Autobiography, My Portfolio Purpose Statement, My Teaching Philosophy, Professional Goals Statement, and Resume. The buttons under "My Work" are organized according to the NAEYC Standards and lead to the work that is evidence of meeting those standards.

## Welcome to my e-Portfolio
## Tanisha Watkins

**About Me**

    My Autobiography

    My Portfolio Purpose Statement

    My Teaching Philosophy

    My Professional Goals

**About My Work and the NAEYC Standards**

    Standard 1

    Standard 2.

    Standard 3

    Standard 4

    Standard 5

    Standard 6

My Showcase Early Childhood Teaching Portfolio will present my best work done while I was a student at Community College and College.
Here you will learn about me, my love for children , my goals , my thoughts about teaching and learning, and the work I have done in becoming a teacher.

**Figure 7-1a: An example of a Welcome Page**

---

About Me

    My Autobiography

    My Portfolio Purpose

    My Teaching Philosophy

    My Professional Goals

About My Work

    Standard 1

    Standard 2

    Standard 3

    Standard 4

    Standard 5

    Standard 6

Insert Welcome Statement Here

**Figure 7-1b: An example of Sketch of the Welcome Page above**

Here are two more examples of Welcome Pages. These are screen shots of actual welcome screens from students' e-portfolios.

**Figure 7-1c: Two screenshot examples of actual e-Portfolio Welcome Pages**

Your storyboard should have plans for the pathways a viewer would take to navigate through your e-portfolio. Here in Fig. 7-2 you will find a tree diagram of a storyboard plan for an entire portfolio.

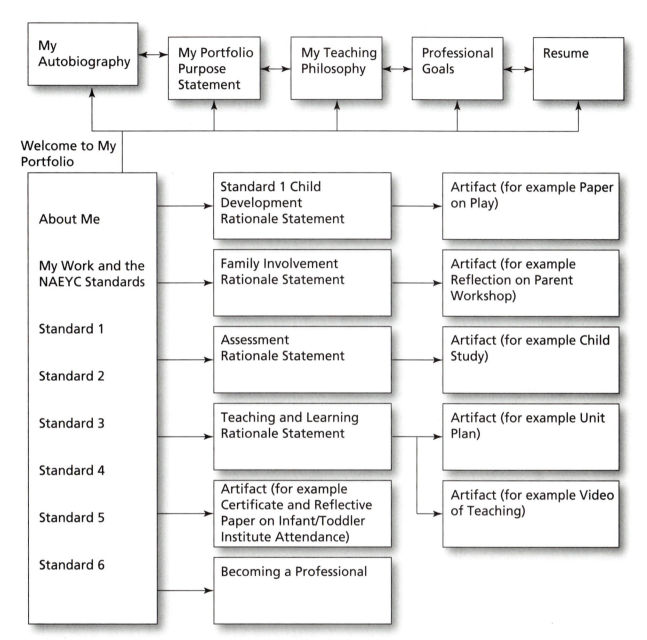

**Figure 7-2: Rough Sketch of "Tree" diagram of Storyboard plan for an e-portfolio**

A navigation template, like the one you see, is one that needs to be planned *perfectly,* because it should clearly direct the viewer to the right place. Here in Fig 7-3 is an example of a sketched plan for part of a navigation page that is clear and gives the viewer the direction needed to get to the student's work. It will lead to the two research papers the student has in the Standard 1 section of her portfolio. When you click "Play Stages, Research Paper on Play in the Toddler Room," you will see the rationale for this paper, when you click the link at the end of the rationale, you will find the paper.

If you map out the path to artifacts in Standard 1, it might look like this:

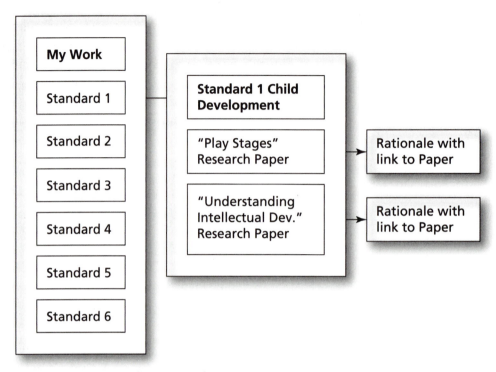

**Figure 7-3: Sketch of Template for Standard 1**

If you are planning the storyboard or pathway for a developmental portfolio with many artifacts, you might want to plan each Standard and its pathway on a single sheet of paper to have room to place all of your artifacts. Here in Figure 7-4 i s a template to use with each standard. Simply enter the number of the template and fill in the name of the artifacts to plan to put in your e-portfolio.

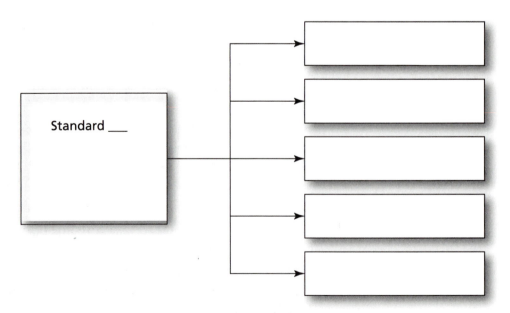

**Figure 7-4: Template for pathway from Standard to artifacts**

Let's begin by creating your storyboard. You want to sketch the templates you will use and the buttons to click to navigate through the presentation. When you sketch, place items such as photos and clip art where you want them. You can sketch in pencil on plain white paper, or you can create a collage using colored paper to represent the buttons.

Figure 7-5 is a template for an e-portfolio with artifacts, if you wish to use paper and pencil. If you have more artifacts, you can add boxes. If you have fewer, simply leave some blank. You can find other versions of templates on our website.

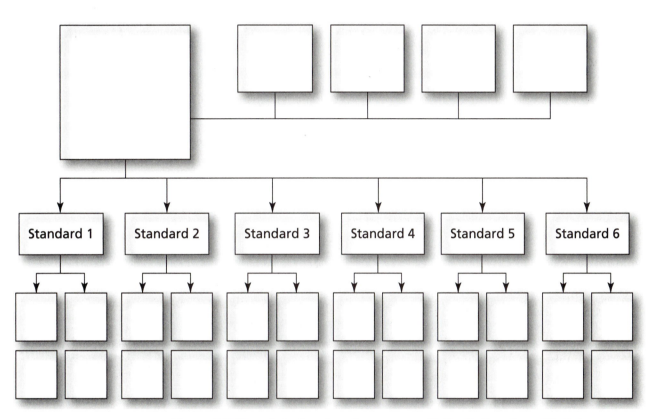

**Figure 7-5: Template for planning an e-portfolio; Rationales with links to artifacts**

You can create your own story pathway, by beginning with your welcome screen box, then proceeding to the next slides you want to present. Sketch in the buttons that will be clicked so that you remember where you want to lead the viewer. Place the arrows where you want the viewer to look next based on what link you have her click. Just plan according to the following steps:

1. Sketch the Welcome screen using the sections in your Table of Contents or navigation buttons, which orients your viewer. This will tell the viewer how you have organized the portfolio.

2. Sketch each branch of the tree that leads to the evidence you are presenting, moving from the Standard to the Rationale to the Artifact(s).

Once you have planned and sketched the pathway for each artifact, you are ready to create your templates (for Microsoft PowerPoint software), or upload artifacts and Rationale Statements to the software your college uses.

## Creating Your Own Sections

You do not have to organize your portfolio using the Standards. If you prefer, your Home page can be organized based on the more general sections this sample student preferred. You will notice in Figure 7-6 the major sections are similar in that she has an "About Me" section with links to her "Welcome Statement," Autobiography, Teaching Philosophy, Professional Goals, and Resume. The second section, "My Work" is divided into the following subsections: Child Development, Curriculum and Teaching, Specialized Coursework, and Professional Development. When you click each subsection you find the work that is organized in that section. For example, in the Child Development section, this student placed papers on "Play." In the Curriculum and Teaching Section she has her rationales that are linked to her lesson plans and unit plans.

---

- ## Welcome to My e-Portfolio

- This e-portfolio traces my work from Infant and Toddler CDA to my Associate's Degree in Early Childhood Education. This is a developmental portfolio so you will share in my journey from its beginning until now. I will share some of my background, my teaching philosophy, my current professional goals, and my work. Although, in the beginning my work had flaws, and I had a lot to learn, over the past two years I have grown in my understanding of child development and teaching. I have attended many professional development workshops and institutes and have certificates in First Aid, Child Abuse and Neglect. My goal is to continue and earn my bachelor's degree in Early Childhood Education.

**About me**
- Welcome
- My Autobiography
- My Teaching Philosophy
- My Professional Goals
- My Resume

**My Work**
- Child Development
- Curriculum and Teaching (Lesson Plans, Unit Plans, Curriculum Projects)
- Related Specialized Coursework Projects
- Research papers
- Professional Development

---

**Figure 7-6: An example of an e-Portfolio organized with general sections (not according to the Standards)**

You can plan whatever organization you prefer. You simply should be sure that it is clear to the reader. You must also be sure that your links lead to the artifacts that you wish to display. As you work on the portfolio, the more you add to it, the easier this process will become. You may find that as you use the software, you will make some changes in your plans. You will become creative using the software adding images, graphics, and artwork that will improve on you plan.

## Assemble Your Portfolio

Now that you have seen two different plans and have planned out your own Welcome screen, you should begin building your e-portfolio. You can write your "Welcome Statement," create your navigation buttons, and add your introductory material (Autobiography, Teaching Philosophy, Professional Goals Statement, Portfolio Purpose Statement, and Resume).

Keep track of each piece of work you collect on the computer by checking it off the Artifact Index sheet. You can see the headings of this sheet:

| Artifact | Rationale Draft/ Completed | Standard or Competency | Selected Yes/No | Collected Computer Check | Uploaded Check |
|---|---|---|---|---|---|

To review how to fill out this form, follow these steps:

1. Enter the name of the item that you are collecting in the first column.

2. Place a check in the Rationale Draft/Completed column when your rationale is in draft form or complete. Jot in the number of the standard or brief note on the competency addressed in the next column.

3. If you select it for your portfolio, write Y for Yes. If you reject it, write N for No.

4. Place a check in the "Uploaded or Entered" Column when you upload it to your server or enter it into your slide presentation.

Once your presentation is completely assembled, you can publish it on your e-portfolio platform or burn it to a CD or DVD, or upload it to your own host server.

### Artifact Index Sheet

| Artifact | Rationale Draft/Completed | Standard or Competency | Selected Yes/No | Collected Computer Check | Uploaded Check |
|---|---|---|---|---|---|
| Welcome Cover Page | | | | | |
| Table of Contents/Navigation | | | | | |
| Portfolio Purpose Statement | | | | | |
| Professional Goals Statement | | | | | |
| Resume (honors) | | | | | |
| Autobiography | | | | | |
| Teaching Philosophy | | | | | |
| Teaching Video | | | | | |
| | | | | | |
| | | | | | |
| | | | | | |
| Transcript(s) | | | | | |
| | | | | | |
| | | | | | |

# Artifact Index Sheet (con't)

| Artifact | Rationale Draft/Completed | Standard or Competency | Selected Yes/No | Collected Computer Check | Uploaded Check |
|---|---|---|---|---|---|
| **Letters of Recommendation** | | | | | |
| | | | | | |
| | | | | | |
| **Standard 1. Promoting Child Development and Learning** | | | | | |
| | | | | | |
| | | | | | |
| **Standard 2. Building Family and Community Relationships** | | | | | |
| | | | | | |
| | | | | | |
| | | | | | |
| **Standard 3. Observing, Documenting, and Assessing to Support Young Children and Families** | | | | | |
| | | | | | |
| | | | | | |
| | | | | | |
| | | | | | |
| **Standard 4. Using Developmentally Effective Approaches to Connect with Children and Families** | | | | | |
| | | | | | |
| | | | | | |
| | | | | | |
| | | | | | |
| **Standard 5. Using Content Knowledge to Build Meaningful Curriculum** | | | | | |
| | | | | | |
| | | | | | |
| | | | | | |
| | | | | | |
| **Standard 6. Becoming a Professional** | | | | | |
| (Certificates) | | | | | |
| | | | | | |
| | | | | | |
| **Miscellaneous** | | | | | |
| | | | | | |
| | | | | | |
| | | | | | |

## Be Aware of Visual Design

Because your documents will be viewed on a computer screen, you must be aware of how they will look as slides on the screen. The first piece you need to design is the Welcome page. If you are working with an e-portfolio software, you will be able to select digital art for a banner, and a digital photo for your welcome screen photo. You might also design your Rationale Statements with a border or a piece of clip art or a photo, which illustrates the work you are presenting. You can do so, as suggested earlier, so that the material seen will signal that it is a Rationale Statement, and so that the entire e-portfolio looks tied together as a whole. In Chapters 5 and 6, there were suggestions and examples of a few Rationale Statements. Remember to be careful to have the design enhance the page and create a sense of continuity with your other work. In other words, if you use a particular border for a rationale statement, you might want to repeat that element with the rest. Or if you use a graphic piece of Word Art to title your Rationale Statement, you might what to use it consistently. In the two first examples below (Fig 7-7a and 7-7b), one student chose to use a digital photo of the children with whom she worked to illustrate her reflection on a Pizza making activity she did. At the end of her reflection, she created a hyperlink to the actual lesson plans for her unit. She also gave a sequence of pictures of her activity with the children making Play dough. By giving the sequence of digital pictures she was able to recreate and illustrate the hands-on lessons, and display her own recipe chart. In the second example (Fig. 7-7c), a student used digital photos from the Internet to illustrate his slide on his Professional Goals Statement with his plans to create a non-profit involved in sports education. As you work on your e-portfolio, you will create your own elements of design that suit you, and which express your voice and point of view.

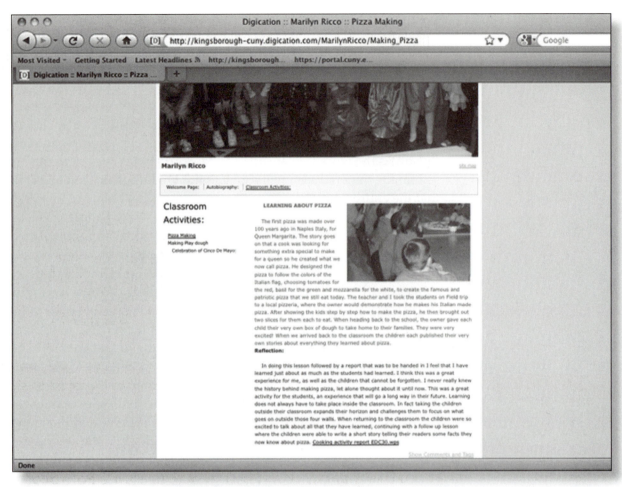

**Marilyn Ricco**

site map

Welcome Page: | Autobiography: | Classroom Activities:

## Classroom Activities:

Pizza Making
Making Play dough
Celebration of Cinco De Mayo:

### LEARNING ABOUT PIZZA

The first pizza was made over 100 years ago in Naples Italy, for Queen Margarita. The story goes on that a cook was looking for something extra special to make for a queen so he created what we now call pizza. He designed the pizza to follow the colors of the Italian flag, choosing tomatoes for the red, basil for the green and mozzarella for the white, to create the famous and patriotic pizza that we still eat today. The teacher and I took the students on field trip to a local pizzeria, where the owner would demonstrate how he makes his Italian made pizza. After showing the kids step by step how to make the pizza, he then brought out two slices for them each to eat. When heading back to the school, the owner gave each child their very own box of dough to take home to their families. They were very excited! When we arrived back to the classroom the children each published their very own stories about everything they learned about pizza.

**Reflection:**

In doing this lesson followed by a report that was to be handed in I feel that I have learned just about as much as the students had learned. I think this was a great experience for me, as well as the children that cannot be forgotten. I never really knew the history behind making pizza, let alone thought about it until now. This was a great activity for the students, an experience that will go a long way in their future. Learning does not always have to take place inside the classroom. In fact taking the children outside their classroom expands their horizon and challenges them to focus on what goes on outside those four walls. When returning to the classroom the children were so excited to talk about all that they have learned, continuing with a follow up lesson where the children were able to write a short story telling their readers some facts they now know about pizza. Cooking activity report EDC30.wps

Show Comments and Tags

Done

---

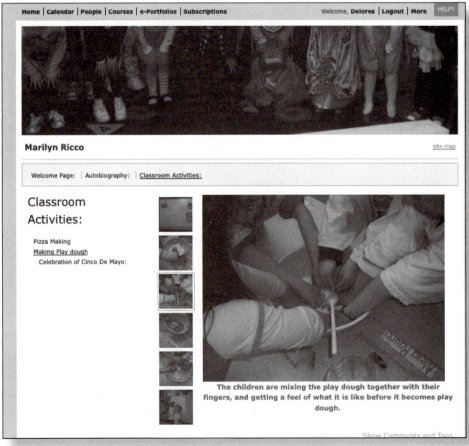

**Marilyn Ricco**

site map

Welcome Page: | Autobiography: | Classroom Activities:

## Classroom Activities:

Pizza Making
Making Play dough
Celebration of Cinco De Mayo:

The children are mixing the play dough together with their fingers, and getting a feel of what it is like before it becomes play dough.

Show Comments and Tags

**Figure 7-7a & 7-7b: Screenshots of an actual e-Portfolio using digital photo of children at work making pizza and playdough**

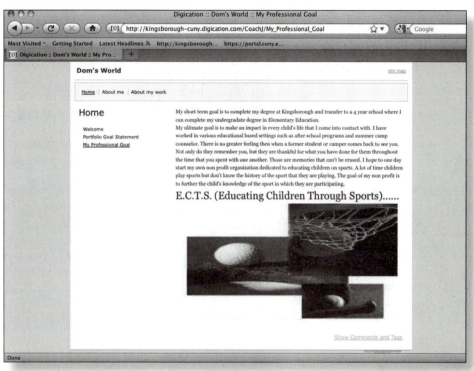

**Figure 7-7c: Screenshot of an actual e-Portfolio using digital art to illustrate Professional Goal Statement**

## Uploading and Linking the Artifacts to Your e-Portfolio

Once all artifacts are digitized and stored in your computer, you are ready to upload them to your e-portfolio. Using your storyboard as a guide, first develop and upload your "Welcome Page." If this contains your navigation buttons, link each of your introductory items (Autobiography, Teaching Philosophy, Goals Statements, and Resume) to the proper buttons. Continue with each item one by one following the storyboard you prepared along the lines of the arrows you drew. If you are using an e-portfolio service they will prompt you to enter your rationales and then to upload your documents. If you are creating your own CD, or DVD, or if you are going to place your own presentation onto a hosting server, assemble the slides of your e-portfolio into a presentation.

Remember, one advantage of creating an e-portfolio, is that you can also create linkages to the web. You can provide links on your rationales to the Standards Summary and the Standard you are citing. Creating links is especially helpful if you have created lessons for children that involved them in research on the web. You might want to have your viewer visit the sites you had researched for children to use. In such an instance once you have described the work in the rationale, you can link to the web address or URL of the website that you have used in your teaching. If you are using e-portfolio software there will be a menu of choices that will allow you to insert a hyperlink. If you are using Power Point to create your own slide or a linking from a word document, you do so by going to the

Insert Menu and selecting Hyperlink. There will be a place for you to enter the website's URL, which will then appear on your page. The viewer can then click the link and will be able to go right to the site you have selected.

If you are using e-portfolio software, your presentation will be presented as a web page, once it is completed and published. Most e-portfolio software has a mechanism for viewing your work as it will appear on the web. When you click on Preview, you will see your presentation as it will appear on the web. You will need to save the presentation as a web page, if you are using Microsoft Word or PowerPoint, by clicking on Save as Web Page below Save As on the File Menu. If you want to see what the image will look like on the web, drag the icon of your presentation slide to your web browser icon and you will see the document as it will appear on the web.

To keep track of the documents you are uploading to the presentation portfolio, use the Artifact Index sheet. You can check the next-to-last column when you have entered the piece into your computer e-portfolio file. If you upload an artifact to the e-portfolio software or enter it into your slide presentation using Power Point, you can then check the last column "uploaded or entered." Uploading your artifacts and your Rationale Statements is the last step in assembling your portfolio. Your navigational page will serve as your "Table of Contents," because it will direct your viewer to the various sections of the portfolio. Check each item off, so that you keep track of each piece and its placement.

## Test the Mechanics

Once you have finished assembling all of the pieces of your portfolio into your portfolio templates, you need to test the mechanics. Many e-portfolio software providers have a way for you to Preview your e-portfolio. You should view the portfolio as though you were an invited guest, navigating your e-portfolio and seeing whether every click leads you to where you want to go. In addition, you want to be sure that once you see the document that you chose to see, you can then come back to the navigation page or the home page. If there are problems, now is the time to correct them.

If you are using an e-portfolio software and service, be sure that you have uploaded all the documents into their proper templates and/ or folders, and that, wherever required, you have a rationale. Once everything works perfectly, you can publish your e-Portfolio.

If you are creating a CD or DVD, once you have put all of your artifacts, links, photos, etc., into the slide presentation, then you can burn the CD or DVD of your work.

## Concluding Remarks

The work you have done in this chapter—preparing your e-portfolio— has prepared you to demonstrate both your skills and abilities as a teacher, and your skills and abilities with technology. As you organized your e-portfolio, you used the computer to collect, organize, and reformat documents. As you constructed your e-portfolio, you uploaded digital images, video, and sound, made hyperlinks to documents, explored the

Internet for resources, engaged in file sharing, and scanned documents into your computer files. All of these skills may not seem extraordinary to you now, because you have been using them to build the e-portfolio, but they are the technology skills of this century. They are the skills that you will be passing on to the children you teach, so that they can create stories and report presentations, and conduct research, using the tools of today. Earlier in this chapter, it was stated that in order to help children to become lifelong learners in today's world we must give them the tools to gather and share information through the use of technology. As early childhood educators, we know that this does not mean replacing play or experiential learning with a computer screen. Children need to play, explore, and interact with each other and with caring adults, to grow and learn. However, the work you have done here shows that you can help to usher this generation of children into the age of technology, so that they can use these technological tools for self-expression and communication, to create, and to invent in this new medium.

## What You Have Accomplished in This Chapter

✔ Explored a variety of examples of e-portfolios;

✔ Explored the process of using templates and creating slides for an e-portfolio presentation;

✔ Collected all of your portfolio artifacts in digital form on your computer;

✔ Organized these portfolio materials into file folders according to the standards;

✔ Created a storyboard or plan for your e-portfolio;

✔ Designed your Welcome page and page for navigating your e-portfolio;

✔ Assembled your e-portfolio slides using your storyboard;

✔ Kept track of your entries using your Artifact Index sheet;

✔ Tested the mechanics of your presentation;

✔ Created a CD or DVD with your e-portfolio;

✔ Published your presentation on the web.

# IV

# Putting it All Together

# Summarizing Thoughts

In this chapter some important considerations you should have applied to your work on your portfolio are summarized. How to create a summarizing document for those who view your portfolio in the form of a brochure is discussed. It ends with some concluding remarks about the process and tying it all together.

## Your Artifacts Are the Heart of Your Portfolio

The most important element of your portfolio is your work and your ideas about your work—in other words, your artifacts themselves and your reflections about them. Your organization and your design are important in as much as they support your work and your reflections on that work. Your reflections hold your work together and give your work meaning. They tell the reader how the work impacted your thinking and your growth. Your artifacts document that growth. Your work, the artifacts and your reflective writing you have created and developed as a teacher, demonstrates what you know, what you can do, and how you think as a teacher.

So, as you review your portfolio, first and foremost be certain that you have selected the best work to represent you as the teacher you are becoming, or the teacher you have become. If it is a developmental portfolio, be certain that all the requisite work required by your program, is compiled. Be certain that the reflections on that work show your thinking about your growth and development. Refer to the syllabi, and note the outcomes the instructors have set out for you, and be sure to cite them in your work when there is evidence of you having achieved the requisite knowledge, strategies, or practices. Your instructors should be able to move through your work, seeing milestones in your development. They should read about your "aha!" moments. The reflections should tell them the story of how the work lead you to the next step in your development, and where you see that work leading you in the future.

If you are creating a showcase portfolio, the work should be your best and be comprehensive. It can be your best for many reasons. It can demonstrate your best talents or areas of giftedness as a teacher in the form of curriculum development, lesson planning, and assessment.

It can stand out because it demonstrates how you drew out excellent work on the part of the children who you taught. It may be your best because it is exemplary research. It may demonstrate excellent connections with parents and families, or show important aspects of advocacy for educational issues. The pieces of work you collect should be comprehensive in that they demonstrate a multifaceted view of who you are as a teacher right now. You want the work to create a rich portrait of you as a teacher and as a professional. Your reflections on that work should show excellent analysis of the work, and an assessment of your skills and abilities, areas of growth, and areas of development to which you aspire.

Your work in the e-portfolio must have a two-fold purpose. Whether it is a developmental portfolio or a showcase portfolio, it should accomplish everything just mentioned, and it must demonstrate your abilities with technology and the Internet. The portfolio should highlight your ability to use the computer and other technological tools to:

- develop documents;
- upload digital images (photos and video) and sound;
- word processing, uploading and downloading files;
- navigate the web;
- compile presentations;
- create hypertext links to the Internet;
- identify resources to your teaching on the Internet;
- help children use Internet resources to do research.

If your e-portfolio highlights these skills and abilities, it should demonstrate that you have developed the skills to help your children to become technologically literate. Every student will have a different level of skill with the computer and technology. All students will not be held to the same standard yet. But your portfolio should demonstrate the best of your work understanding and using technology in building your portfolio, and in the skills you can pass on to children.

As you look over your portfolio, first focus on the work. Use the following check list to look for these things.

## Developmental Portfolio Checklist

In the developmental portfolio, does the work show your growth and development in:

_____ Knowledge about child development

_____ Assessing development

_____ Developing curriculum (planning activities and units)

_____ Working with parents and the community

_____ Developing as a professional

## Showcase Portfolio Checklist

In the showcase portfolio, does your work show the best of your work in:

_____ Knowledge about child development

_____ Assessing development

_____ Developing curriculum (planning activities and units)

_____ Working with parents and the community

_____ Developing as a professional

## E-portfolio Checklist

In the electronic portfolio, does your work show your progress in the aforementioned areas *and* does it show your ability to:

_____ Create documents

_____ Research using the Internet

_____ Use resources from the Internet in your teaching

_____ Use technology and the computer

_____ Professionally develop technology skills and abilities related to teaching

## Tying it Together with Summarizing Documents

As you look through your portfolio, you should have a sense that the artifacts and reflections have some cohesion. They should be tied together through the themes of your beliefs and principles. If you look back at your Teaching Philosophy, the guiding principles, which you hold dear, and the values, which you practice in your teaching, can help provide you with the threads that should run through the portfolio and create a sense of connectedness for the reader. Here are a few examples of the threads that can run through a student's work and create a sense that the work ties together.

For example, if you wrote in your Teaching Philosophy Statement about the importance of experiential learning and autonomy and independence for young children, then the activities that you highlight in your section on teaching and learning may demonstrate hands-on learning activities with children engaged in inquiry developing their own questions and collecting data. If you have experienced practical hands-on work in the classroom in a few different age groups, your reflections might give examples of differing levels of understandings children might gain from experiential learning in a Pre-K, kindergarten, or primary grade classroom. Or, if you highlight the importance of supporting the young child's development of autonomy, you may want to highlight activities that give them choices. You may want to highlight work you have done to share information on development and autonomy with parents. You might highlight special workshops you have taken learning about the "Terrible Twos" with your reflections on the lessons learned.

You may want to highlight or draw attention to the themes in your portfolio by creating a summarizing document. It can be a brief statement with a few bullets. It can also be a brochure, which is a bit longer but highlights the main aspects of your portfolio. For a binder portfolio, you can simply include a note to the reader. Sometimes the themes in your work are obvious to you. Sometimes you have to reflect on your portfolio to find the themes. Reflect on your work with the following questions.

---

**REFLECTIONS ON MY PORTFOLIO**

1. What recurring values and beliefs appear in my work?
2. What strong interests or abilities seem to resonate in different pieces of my work?
3. What are my proudest moments evidenced in my work to become a teacher?

---

Once your have identified the themes that run through your work, you can create a summarizing document that calls the reader's attention to these themes. You can use sticky note-style flags to call attention to the work you wish to highlight. Any brightly colored flags with an arrow pointing to the work to be highlighted will do the trick.

Here is an example:

---

Dear Reader,

In my journey to becoming a teacher, I have developed a few interests that I would like to highlight for you here. I am very interested in developing **literacy** and the **love of good children's books,** and the involvement of parents in the education of their children. I have, therefore, flagged for you:

- Learning activities for Pre-K and Kindergarten in language and literacy (flagged in green);

- An annotated bibliography of children's books I have developed (flagged in red);

- Parent involvement activities (flagged in blue);

  — The Head Start Parent Newsletter I developed;

  — Two Parent Workshops to which I contributed ("Loving Books," "Planting Seeds and Watching Them Grow").

---

What you are attempting to do is draw connections between the pieces of work in the portfolio for the reader and flag them so they are not missed. This will guide him or her through the work, and support the understanding of your strengths and talents, and the work that you value, because you have set out the roadmap to follow as a guide to the examination of your work.

If you have difficulty seeing the themes in your work, discuss your work with your peers, and your professors, instructors, or directors. Read through the comments that have been written on your work to find out what the professors felt your strengths were, and what you value seems to emerge.

## A Professional Presentation for Your Binder

A minor note here on the presentation of your binder portfolio. You spent a great deal of time creating, organizing, and designing your portfolio. If you go on an interview and bring it with you, consider carrying it in a professional-looking tote—not a shopping bag. Binder portfolios, especially developmental portfolios are too big and bulky to fit in a briefcase, so an alternative is a professional looking tote. A tote bag obtained at an educational conference, or a professional-looking one you purchase will do the trick. It will also show that you value your work and your portfolio.

### Portfolio Brochure

Another way to tie together the themes in your portfolio for the reader is to prepare a brochure of your work, which in essence presents your portfolio to a reader. A brochure can let a potential reader of your portfolio know that you have a portfolio, the form it takes (binder, CD, DVD, Internet address for your e-portfolio), its purpose and some of the themes or organizing principles that guided you in your work.

You can send a brochure to a potential employer to introduce yourself and to preview the ideas and the work in your portfolio. It has the added benefit of demonstrating a certain level of computer skill. Most word-processing programs have templates that make developing a brochure quite easy.

We have included an example of a brochure for a student who has just completed her four-year degree after having begun her college work in a Community College and working in a Head Start Center.

You will note that on the cover flap she has an attractive photo, and information on where she can be reached. The first inside flap tells you about her teaching philosophy and the practices she values. The inside last flap discusses threads of her work tying it all together. The back left flap talks about her experience. The back center tells how to access her portfolio, her e-mail address, and telephone number. So in the one trifold document there is a taste of her portfolio designed to have the reader say, "I'd like to see the whole portfolio and meet this candidate."

A brochure is a public relations tool for you and your portfolio. It should tie together the themes that have emerged in your portfolio, and a snapshot about you and your work in one cohesive document.

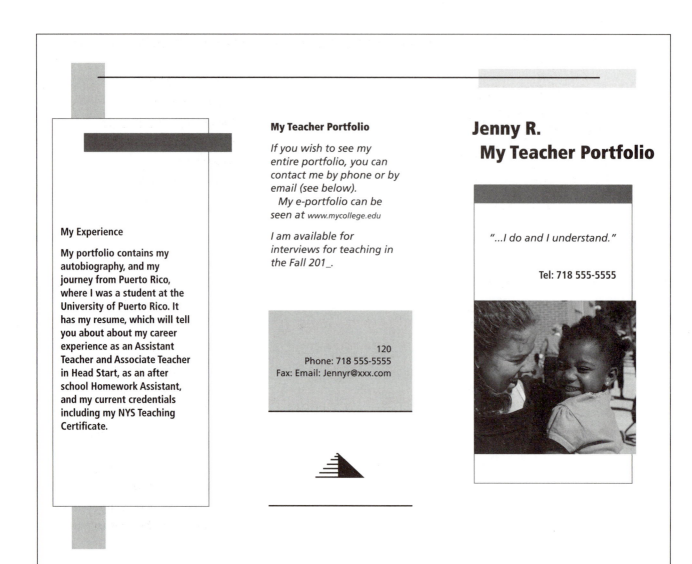

My Teacher Portfolio

*If you wish to see my entire portfolio, you can contact me by phone or by email (see below).*
*My e-portfolio can be seen at www.mycollege.edu*

*I am available for interviews for teaching in the Fall 201_.*

120
Phone: 718 55S-5555
Fax: Email: Jennyr@xxx.com

Jenny R.
My Teacher Portfolio

*"...I do and I understand."*

Tel: 718 555-5555

My Experience

My portfolio contains my autobiography, and my journey from Puerto Rico, where I was a student at the University of Puerto Rico. It has my resume, which will tell you about about my career experience as an Assistant Teacher and Associate Teacher in Head Start, as an after school Homework Assistant, and my current credentials including my NYS Teaching Certificate.

## Concluding Remarks

As you see your portfolio coming to fruition, you should be filled with pride in your accomplishment. Although receiving your degree or certification as a teacher are symbols of your accumulated work to become a teacher, your portfolio is the representation of that goal fulfilled. It is, in the case of the developmental portfolio, all of the small steps that you took along the journey to the goal of becoming a teacher. In the case of the showcase, it is your major giant steps toward that goal. In the case of the e-portfolio, it is also the evidence of your learning to become a teacher and to attain the knowledge of technology that will launch your students into the information age.

If you have a binder portfolio, you can feel the weight of your work in your hand. As you flip through the pages, you will remember the late night struggles with a particular piece of work. You will recall the children whose lives you touched and who touched yours. As you

**My Showcase Portfolio**

highlights my work and supports my Teaching Philosophy, and my values and beliefs in the following:

- Experiential learning;

- the Power of Good Children's Literature in the Curriculum;

- Inquiry-based learning;

- the Importance of Parent Involvement.

**My Showcase Portfolio**

highlights my work at

_____

related to the NAEYC Standards:

- Promoting Child Development

- Building Family and Community Relationships

- Assessment

- Teaching and Learning

- Professional Development

**A Preview of My Work**

**Child Development**

**Research papers on child development theory**

**Assessment**

**Kindergarten Child Study**

**Teaching and Learning**

**Units in language and literacy including:**

- **Lessons based on children's literature;**

- **Math and Science lessons based on cooking;**

- **Room arrangement projects with floor plans and photographs of area organization for pre-kindergarten.**

**Building Family Relationships including:**

- **My contributions to a Parent Newsletter;**

- **Parent workshop ideas that I have helped to develop.**

skim through the templates or slides of your e-portfolio, you may see children's photos of photos of their work, and recall the impact of your lessons on the children who you were privileged to teach. Take the time to enjoy those feelings. Reflect on those feelings. Capture them on paper—not necessarily to place them in the portfolio, but to mark this time as a teacher. Endings are important to teachers because they prepare you to move ahead. When you stop and take stock of where you are, what you have learned, and how you feel about what you have learned, you prepare yourself to begin again.

A portfolio at this juncture may feel to you as though it is finished, but in fact it is a dynamic tool and resource as you continue your career as an early childhood professional. As you progress in your teaching, you will refer back to the units and lessons you have documented as a resource, for ideas for teaching. You will add new ideas, materials, and evidence of student work that represents the current work you have achieved. You might take pieces of work out, file them, and replace them with materials that relate to your current teaching assignment.

*I bumped into a student who had long graduated from community college, and told her I was doing a book on portfolios and asked if she recalled hers, and would talk to me about her memories. She said, "I still have it. I use it all the time. When the principal placed me in third grade, I took out my pre-k stuff but I kept some of my first grade lessons, and my beginning reading activities. I keep the things I take out in my file cabinet. I got this job, because of my portfolio. So it just keeps growing and changing."*

So take the time to reflect a bit on this moment in time. Think about your accomplishments. Reflect on the work as a whole as it is collected here. Reflect on the process of documenting this journey to becoming a teacher.

## Reflections on Portfolio Development

1. What have I learned about myself from developing this portfolio?

2. What have I learned from the children I have encountered?

3. What have I learned from the colleagues and mentors with whom I have worked?

4. Where do I want to take this portfolio in the future?

## Final Thoughts

Your portfolio will serve you as a teacher by becoming a resource, a source of inspiration, and a reminder of your abilities as a teacher. It can become a growing, changing testament to who you are as a teacher. The time and care you have put into its development will be paid back in dividends that you can never fully measure. It will fill you with pride. It will speak of your talents and abilities and help you build a career. It will help you to reflect and assess your work, so that you can move to the next level. It will propel you to meet your future goals. Take a moment to savor those notions, because they represent a significant milestone in your journey to become a teacher.

# References

Barrett, Helen. 2000. Create your own electronic portfolio. *Learning & Leading with Technology* (27)7, 14–21.

Barrett, Helen. 2000. Electronic portfolios. In *Educational Technology; An Encyclopedia* Santa Barbara, CA: ABC-CLIO, http://electronicportfolios .com/portfolios/encyclopediaentry.htm (accessed January 3, 2008).

Barrett, Helen. 2000. Electronic teaching portfolios: Multimedia skills + portfolio development = powerful professional development. Association for the Advancement of Computing in Education (AACE). Distributed via the Web by permission of AACE. http://electronicportfolios.org/ portfolios/site2000.html (accessed March, 2009).

Barrett, Helen. 2006. Digital stories in ePortfolios: Multiple purposes and tools. http://electronicportfolios.org/digistory/purposesmac.html#intro (accessed August 30, 2009).

Barrett, Helen (2010). "Blurring the boundaries: Social networking & ePortfolio development." YouTube video. TEDxASB (India). February 25, 2010. http://www.youtube.com/watch?v=ckcSegrwjkA

Barrett, Helen. (n.d.). Electronic portfolios.org. http://electronicportfolios .org/ (accessed August 20, 2008).

Bredekamp, S. (Ed.). 1987. *Developmentally appropriate practice in early childhood programs serving children from birth through age 8,* expanded edition. Washington, DC: National Association for the Education of Young Children.

Brookfield, S. 1995. *Becoming a critically reflective teacher.* San Francisco, CA: Jossey-Bass.

Dewey, J. 1944. *Democracy and education.* New York: The Free Press.

Finger, G., McGlasson, M., and Finger, P. 2006. "Developing an ePortfolio approach: stories of personal learning." Paper presented at The Australian Computers in Education Conference 2006, Cairns, Australia, October 2–4, 2006. http://www98.griffith.edu.au/dspace/ bitstream/10072/11745/1/41219.pdf (accessed January 07, 2008).

International Society for Technology in Education (ISTE). 2008. The ISTE National Education Technology Standards and Performance Indicators for Teachers (NETS-T). Retrieved October 30, 2010, from http://www.iste.org/Libraries/PDFs/NETS_for_Teachers_2008_EN.sflb.ashx

International Society for Technology in Education (ISTE). 2007. The ISTE National Education Teaching Standards and Performance Indicators for Students (NETS-S). Retrieved October 30, 2010, from http://www.iste.org/Libraries/PDFs/NETS_for_Student_2007_EN.sflb.ashx

Interstate New Teacher Assessment and Support Consortium. 1992. *Model standards for beginning teacher licensing, assessment and development: A resource for state dialogue.* Washington, DC: Council of Chief State School Officers. http://www.ccsso.org/content/pdfs/corestrd.pdf (accessed January 3, 2009).

Kolb, A. and Kolb, D. (2005). Learning styles and learning spaces: Enhancing experiential learning in higher education. *Academy of Management Learning & Education*, 4(2), 193–212.

LaGuardia Community College. (n.d.). e-Portfolio gallery. http://www.eportfolio.lagcc.cuny.edu/showcase_gallery.html (accessed May, 2009).

NAEYC. 2003. *Standards for early childhood professional preparation associate degree programs.* Washington, DC: Author. http://www.naeyc.org/files/naeyc/file/positions/2003.pdf (accessed January 15, 2008).

NAEYC. 2009. *Where we stand on standards for programs to prepare early childhood professionals.* Washington, DC: Author. www.naeyc.org/files/positions/programStandards.pdf (accessed April, 2010).

NAEYC, 2009. NAEYC Standards for Early Childhood Professional Preparation Programs. Washington, D.C.: Author. http://www.naeyc.org/files/naeyc/file/positions/ProfPrepStandards09.pdf (accessed August, 2010).

National Board for Professional Teaching Standards. 2009. "Early childhood generalist assessment at a glance." Prepared by Pearson for National Board for Professional Teaching Standards. http://www.nbpts.org/userfiles/File/EC_Gen_AssessAtaGlance.pdf (accessed April, 2009).

Paulson, F. L., Paulson, P. R., and Meyer, C. A. 1991. What makes a portfolio? Eight thoughtful guidelines will help educators encourage self-directed learning. *Educational Leadership,* 48(5), 60–63. copyright EBSCO Publishing, 2003, http://faculty.milkenschool.org/sperloff/edtech/portfolioarticle2.pdf (accessed March, 2010).

Paulson, P. R. and Paulson, F. L. 1991. Portfolios: Stories of knowing. Paper presented at the 54th Claremont Reading Conference, March, 1991. Eric document. http://eric.ed.gov/ERICDocs/data/ericdocs2sql/content_storage_01/0000019b/80/13/79/09.pdf (accessed January, 2009).

Reed, J. and Koliba, C. 2003. "Facilitating reflection: A manual for leaders and educators." John Dewey Project on Progressive Education, University of Vermont. http://www.uvm.edu/~dewey/reflect.pdf (accessed January, 2009).

Schön, D. A. 1987. Teaching artistry through reflection-in-action. In *Educating the reflective practitioner,* 22–40. San Francisco, CA: Jossey-Bass.

Westberg, J. and Jason, H. 2001. *Fostering reflection and providing feedback: Helping others learn from experience.* New York: Springer Publishing.

# Index